THE READER ORGANISATION

NEWS AND EVENTS

'FROM BETTER TO BEST': THE READER ORGANISATION LEADS LIVERPOOL READING CAMPAIGN

The Reader Organisation has been chosen as official partner in Mayor Joe Anderson's campaign to make Liverpool the UK's foremost literate city and ensure every child leaves primary school a reader. We were highlighted as an example of best practice in 'From Better to Best', a new report published by Liverpool Education Commission, and have since been commissioned to lead the initiative to raise educational standards in the city.

The Reader Organisation's shared-reading projects with young people focus entirely on reading for pleasure, something that the Organisation for Economic Co-operation and Development research has highlighted as the most important factor affecting a child's social mobility. Not only do young people who read with us develop a love of reading, but they improve their literacy, wellbeing, and social skills. We are delighted to be working with the Mayor and local schools to get Liverpool's children reading.

SHARED READING FOR HEALTHY COMMUNITIES

The Reader Organisation held their third national conference, Shared Reading for Healthy Communities, at the British Library on May 16th. The conference brought together professionals from health, education, social care, criminal justice and libraries to explore how our pioneering shared reading project addresses the need for social inclusion, meaningful activity and better health in communities across the UK and beyond.

Headline speaker Andy Burnham MP, Shadow Secretary for Health, movingly discussed 'The Books that Built Me' with Jane Davis, highlighting the poetry of Tony Harrison as a particular influence. Other panellists debated 'Finding a New Language for Mental Health', 'Living Well with Dementia' and 'Reading and Recovery'.

THE READER ORGANISATION ONLINE

The Reader Organisation's website has been redesigned with a new look and lots of new features. There's more information about our activities and it's now easier than ever to purchase copies of The Reader and our anthologies. See for yourself at www.thereader.org.uk. We're also on Twitter: @thereaderorg.

CONTENTS

JOSEPH MARCELL AS KING LEAR
IN A TOURING PRODUCTION BY
SHAKESPEARE'S GLOBE

(MANSION HOUSE GARDEN THEATRE,
CALDERSTONES PARK
AUGUST 13–14)

NEW WRITING / BOOK TALK / NEWS AND REVIEWS

THE READER

No. 51 AUTUMN 2013

Published by The Reader Organisation

EDITOR   Philip Davis

DEPUTY EDITOR   Sarah Coley
CO-EDITORS   Elizabeth Cain
                           Angela Macmillan
                           Eleanor McCann
                           Brian Nellist

ADDRESS   The Reader Magazine
                           The Reader Organisation
                           The Friary Centre
                           Bute Street
                           Liverpool
                           L5 3LA

EMAIL   magazine@thereader.org.uk
WEBSITE   www.thereader.org.uk
BLOG   www.thereaderonline.co.uk

DISTRIBUTION   See p. 128

COVER IMAGE   Michael Troy, Artist and Illustrator,
                           'Little Comfort', watercolour

ISBN 978-0-9576683-0-0

SUBMISSIONS

The Reader genuinely welcomes submissions of poetry, fiction, essays, readings and thought. We publish professional writers and absolute beginners. Send your manuscript with SAE please to:

The Reader Organisation, The Friary Centre, Bute Street, Liverpool, L5 3LA

Printed and bound in the European Union by Bell and Bain Ltd, Glasgow

EDITORIAL

'WHILE I... UNMOVED, UNKNOWING'

THOMAS HARDY, 'THE GOING'

Philip Davis

Boswell would eagerly ask Samuel Johnson on sundry occasions whether he had read such-and-such a book. To which Johnson would often reply, 'Sir, I have looked into it.' That was Johnson, the rough literary man, impatiently manhandling the latest books, ripping the heart and mind out of them as quickly as he could. Today I have been 'looking into' a book on the Victorian novel called *Thinking without Thinking*, partly because it had a bad review by a hot-tempered reviewer called Currie in *TLS* (itself a recommendation as far as I am concerned), but mainly because of its title. Not to judge books by covers, but on occasions the titles can be more like little lines of poetry than adverts, and sometimes indeed they have more thought in them than the rest of the book. I bought John Burnside's (actually very fine) collection of short stories, *Something Like Happiness* recently because of that word 'like'.

I love the idea of thinking without thinking. The child psychologist Piaget showed that we do not need to know *how* we carry out a task, however complex, for it to be successful. The more that people become experts in a given field, the more their knowledge becomes personal and embodied rather than transmittable by explicit rules. It is great when something is so implicitly and deeply known that you work *from* it rather than have to know *about* it. It feels like life itself, the person in his or her own element, implicit thinking enfolded in the action it serves. Everyone must have experienced cases when the absorption in an effort does not seem consciously to be effortful, precisely because of the immersion of attention. Take even a hard walk to a desired destination: it is better than going to the gym for health's sake. The very effort in how to get there, like the knowledge of how to do the getting, is absorbed in the end for which effort and knowledge are no more than largely unthinking means *en route*. This gain in implicit thinking is the best way to learn – when you are really in pursuit of what the learning leads you towards.

But *Thinking without Thinking* is also about a phenomenon in the Victorian novel which the professionals call Free Indirect Discourse. It happens when a novelist no longer says directly of his character: 'He thought he would go to see her and explain the whole terrible business.' Instead the novelist writes, 'He would go to see her, he would explain…' Though still writing from the third person (*he* and *her*), it is as though the novelist has actually got under the skin, into the semiconscious mind, of the first person at a level deeper and subtler than explicit intention ('I will go and see her. I will explain'). This great simple tool is the way in which the Victorian novel allows its reader to get into the unknown world – all those unspoken thoughts and feelings hidden in the people all around you, half-separated from each other even in their connections. Theirs are not even thoughts that the characters necessarily know they are having. They are messages sometimes secret even to those who are transmitting them – thoughts denied, motives obscured, things never to be spoken out loud and confessed in the outer world even though known, indirectly, in the tacit language of the realist novel.

But it has also made me think of all the things I haven't thought of, of all the times I didn't seem to be thinking and yet now vividly recall. Over the last year or so for example (and as usual I make apology for the state of mental health this reveals), I have had recurrent thoughts and snatched dreams about a terrible event that occurred when I was at university, nearly forty years ago, which I would have said I had never much thought about then or later. Two or three students shared rooms on the top floor of a high accommodation block in college. In party mood, they would have some daft game in which they would step out of the window and stand on the ledge, God knows how many feet high above the walkways. One night whilst one of the friends was skylarking out on the ledge, another shut the window for a joke. The boy outside fell to his death.

It was a horror that happened, and particularly horrifying amidst a small college community. But I don't remember thinking much about it, perhaps in some sort of desperate denial rather than heartlessness, I hope. Only now I recurrently think of what the boy who fell might have thought in the split second the window shut him out. And, more, I involuntarily imagine what the boy who shut the window must have thought the moment after he slammed it shut and felt and heard the consequence. Also, though I don't know his name and have never met him since, what he must have thought of that instant for all the rest of his own life.

There are undoubtedly better things to rescue from the varieties of unthinkingness. One is the delight I have had in being absorbed with and in children, now grandchildren, and their involvement in the joy of their moments. 'I *did* it' is one of the favourite sentences I hear in their excited tones of achievement. An older girl walks down the street staring at the certificate of achievement she is carrying home at the end of her first year in the big school: she does not notice me looking at her, her inner smile all delighted self-amazement. I *did* it, as the guilty have also to say.

But this is a sad week in which I lost my innocent friend Martin Boston to sudden, unexpected death, on holiday in Toronto whilst, of course, we did not know back home. This issue sees what was to have been the launch of an occasional series by him on his life in music. He told me he wrote the pieces on his recent retirement mainly for his daughters, and we carry on printing the first of these as planned in this issue – which, meant to be back to normal after our fiftieth, itself is now to be dedicated to his memory. I don't look up a Stanley Middleton poem we published, I think, time past in issue 34: 'God / knows my friend has died.'

EDITOR'S PICKS

New poetry from **Hannah Lowe, John Wedgwood Clarke, Jonathan Edwards**, and **Barney Eden**. **Jean Sprackland**, who gives us a wonderfully precarious poem, 'Taking Down the Scaffolding', is also featured in Charlie Darby-Villis's account of her visit to HMP Low Newton.

In Poet on His Work, **Seán Haldane** writes on the strange arrangement of personal time in his poem 'Privel Da Crappa!'

New fiction comes from **Stuart Evers** with 'What's Going on Outside?', a bleak and then marvellously not-bleak story about immigrant experience, and from **Victoria Benn** in whose story 'Urchin', Tomi, a Japanese/Australian boy struggles to belong.

At the heart of the issue, in 'Four Helpings of Hardy', we invite **Mike Irwin, Bernard O'Donoghue, Jane Thomas** and **Josie Billington** to pick and discuss favourite poems from Thomas Hardy. These brief essays give sharp moments of focus on the poet's craft, nature and beliefs.

Frances Macmillan, the new Vintage Classics editor is interviewed on publishing matters and the *Stoner* phenomenon. You will also find combative, engaging and fascinating essays from **Philip Davis, Martin Boston** and **Malcolm Bennett**. There are bees and butterflies in this issue.

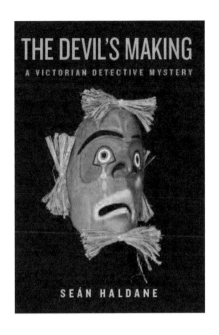

THE DEVIL'S MAKING:
A VICTORIAN DETECTIVE MYSTERY

Victoria, 1869. Vastly outnumbered by native 'Indians', a few thousand British, American, European, and Chinese settlers aspire to the values of the Victorian age.
In the forest a mutilated body is discovered…

"Goes way beyond ordinary genre novels. Haldane integrates human drama with the setting, which he knows like the back of his hand."
Tom Henighan

Stone Flower Press with Rún Press
ISBN 978-0991907304; £11.99

TWO BOOKS BY SEÁN HALDANE
poet and neuropsychologist

TIME / NO TIME:
THE PARADOX OF POETRY AND PHYSICS

The first theoretical physicist, Parmenides, also a poet, described how change cannot logically exist yet it observably exists. This kind of paradox is the stuff of poetry. Since the arrival of quantum physics it is the stuff of physics too.
This book explores the findings of neuroscience as well as the experience of poets and physicists when faced with the paradox of *Time / No Time*.

Parmenides Books
ISBN 978-0957466906; £11.99

THE POET ON HIS WORK

ON 'PRIVEL DA CRAPPA!'

Seán Haldane

PRIVEL DA CRAPPA!

One thing falls from another – like falling rocks:
The signs PRIVEL DA CRAPPA! caught in the headlights
As we careened down forest roads from the Stelvio
(DANGER OF ROCKS!) We lay that night
Chastely back to back in a single bed.
We had first kissed the week before, as meteors fell
Over olive groves and cypresses – Notte di San Lorenzo.

Tonight is San Lorenzo. I've been reading a book
About Rumantsch: PRIVEL DA CRAPPA!
I'm using the pepper grinder I bought in Florence
That summer we came together without coming,
Not knowing all would come to nothing
And we would fall hurtling down the bends
Of time screaming without a sound.

What would we live? – lust
Falling out of love. But when did we fall in?
Were we not just good friends?
Wasn't that the trouble?
What were the fragments in the eventual rubble?
Lust, friendship, hope? It was hope
That drove us down that perilous slope.

No meteors now: the night sky is dull with haze
And we are living out our days
On separate continents. The peppercorns are ground,
Fall to dust.

SEÁN HALDANE

This poem is about my time with an American girl (I'll call her K) I met in Florence when we were both very young, which started in hope but by a couple of years later was 'on the rocks' and ended sadly. But I don't deliberately write poems 'about' things. In a recent book about what I call 'the paradox of poetry and physics' I describe how poems are often the last link in a chain of what Robert Graves called 'more-than-coincidence'. They just happen.

This one happened last year on 10th August which the Italians call San Lorenzo and is known for its annual meteor shower. I had realised in the morning that it was San Lorenzo and I looked forward to watching the shooting stars with my wife, but as I was preparing supper I realised the cloud-cover was too dense. I found myself thinking of when K and I went for a drive up into the hills (49 years before!) and walked under the moon among cypress trees, not knowing it was San Lorenzo, then the shooting stars began to fall. Now I had been reading a book by a friend which he had just sent me from Switzerland, called *Muintir Sleibhe agus A Teanga* (*People of the Mountains and their Language*) which is, of all things, a study written in Irish Gaelic about another unusual language, Rumantsch. I had found myself thinking that although somewhere I had an old anthology of Rumantsch poetry called *Musa Rumantscha*, the only words I could now remember in Rumantsch were 'PRIVEL DA CRAPPA'. I had seen them on signs when K and I had driven together to Switzerland where she had to meet up with her parents and where I was going to see a friend. Careening down from the Stelvio Pass and having to swerve as the headlights lit up rocks in the road but sometimes hitting them, we had joked about how funny it was that 'crappa' must mean 'rocks' – like lumps of 'crap'. They must have done some damage since the car's temperature gauge began to shoot up and when we reached the bottom of the pass late at night we stopped at a garage where there was a light. The garage owner said he would fix the car in the morning and, thinking we were married, gave us a room to sleep in.

Now my realisation that it would be too cloudy to see the stars, and the coincidence of thinking of San Lorenzo and Rumantsch, somehow started the poem, and as it came pushing into my head I also realised I was holding in my hand an old pepper-pot I had bought in Florence that summer of 1963. I went and wrote the poem down – more or less as it stands, although I repeated the phrase 'PRIVEL DA CRAPPA' four times and on revision cut this down to two. The pepper pot entered in, and I saw in my mind the peppercorns like crumbling rocks. And I 'flashed' on an Italian film I had seen a few years ago about an old man and old woman who at last make love on San Lorenzo's night. I felt painfully old.

So the poem is an example of the process in which a poem is the last event in a 'series', or a chain of more-than-coincidence. It also, like many poems, has various layers of meaning that I only became aware of as I was writing it down. As usual, I didn't know what the poem was 'about' until it ended. And as usual, there are unwritten phrases somehow in the background. The relationship eventually went 'on the rocks'. It went 'down hill'. I did not at the time see the 'danger' of our painful future. I couldn't see around the bends. And poems I have written 'to', or as the Elizabethans would say 'through' K have often been set in mountains. The following year we lived for a while in the Italian Alps – and we used to listen to people singing Alpine songs in the local Inn, and I became interested in the whole Alpine culture which cuts across Italian, Rumantsch and German.

This poem has not been published until now. I wonder if it is too eccentric, too self-referential. Also perhaps too gloomy, but although 'one thing falls from another', like the rocks from the crumbling mountains, things fall together in the poem and it is alive. I am glad the poem is in *The Reader*. But I have to say it was not written for anyone but myself and the Muse, and perhaps K if she ever reads it, and those who I know like my poems. If a few other people read it and get something out of it then I'll be very pleased.

I don't believe in 'glossing' poems whether by adding footnotes or by explaining them in prose. A poem is a whole different way of looking at things. It may tell a story, but not as prose does. I can certainly add information to the poem, as I have just done here, which fills out the story into something more like a prose narrative – thinner, more discursive, more rational. But the point of the poem is itself. Its world is 'feeling thought'. Although it forced itself on me as I was preparing supper, wearing an apron, pepper-pot in hand, I was moved by it. If it moves you, or touches you, then I suppose that at some level the story or part of it is yours as well as mine – humanly ours.

STUART EVERS

© AIDAN
JACKSON

FICTION

WHAT'S GOING ON OUTSIDE?

Stuart Evers

Karel sat at the card table peeling his third orange. His hands were large and powerful, his fingers nimble and dextrous. By the time he'd finished, the flesh of the orange was clean, pithless and perfectly round. For a short time he admired his handiwork then split the orange into segments. He ate them with such speed it suggested he feared a piece might be stolen. When done, he sucked the juice from the fingers of his left hand, and with his right removed another orange from the plastic sack at his feet.

'For the love of God, Karel,' Eugene said. 'How many oranges can one man eat?'

Karel looked up from his fourth orange, his nail already under the peel. The older man – canted, pocked face, grey eyed – was stretched out on the right-hand bed, a newspaper just below his eyes.

'Would you like one?' Karel said. 'I have plenty.'

'Speak Russian, Karel!' Eugene said. 'It's almost midnight. It's much too late in the day for English.'

'Would you like one?' Karel said in Russian. 'I have plenty.'

'You know I can't abide oranges,' Eugene said. 'You know I can't even stand the way you peel your oranges. So just be quiet, okay? Be quiet and eat your fucking oranges.'

The answer was nine: one man – or at least the one who was Karel – could eat nine oranges in one sitting. The last two are not pleasant: too sweet by that point, too sticky on the fingers no matter how many times you might wash them. And their room was the furthest away from both bathroom and kitchen. Those last two oranges were something like an ordeal; but Karel always liked to push things. That's what his father said. And Eugene too.

'Does it not give you a stomach ache?' Eugene asked, setting aside his newspaper and tapping a cigarette against the wall.

'They're on special offer downstairs,' he said. 'The girl gives me a discount too. They're good oranges. They're good for you,' he said and looked at Eugene the way he always did when Eugene lit a cigarette.

'Nothing is good for you,' Eugene said. 'Everything's going to kill you one day. You're so young you can't even see that.'

'You're so old,' Karel said. 'You can't even hear how sad you sound.'

Eugene picked up the newspaper, moved from the bed to the window. It was a broken sash, three floors up. They had the best room because Eugene had been there longest and got to choose his roommate and where he slept. When he'd first arrived, he'd shared a bedroom with five other men, sleeping in shifts, the smells and noises like cattle. Now there was a wardrobe and a dresser, a card table and two single beds, a window out of which to look.

Karel ate his orange and picked out another.

'What's going on outside?' Karel asked.

The room was above a green-grocers and the view was down onto the main road. The shops were Turkish, Kurdish, Greek; open all hours. There was always something to see, either down at street level or in the flats and bedsits above. In the smaller window at one o'clock to them, a man was jigging a small child up and down. He wasn't wearing anything on his top half and was animatedly singing as he bounced the child around.

'There are a few lights on. The man with the baby's there.'

'No ladies tonight?'

'No ladies, no.' Eugene said.

'There never are any ladies, are there?'

'No. They're all such *teases*, aren't they?' Eugene said.

* * *

Karel sat at the card table peeling his tenth orange. His hands were large and powerful, his fingers nimble and dextrous despite their stickiness. By the time he'd finished, the flesh of the orange was almost-pithless. He split the orange into segments and ate them with such speed it suggests he feared a piece might be stolen. When done, he sucked the juice from the fingers of his left hand, and with his right removed another orange from the plastic sack at his feet.

'And you're just going to sit there, are you?' Eugene said. 'Eating your oranges? Eating one after another?'

The tenth one tasted of nothing; the eleventh one the same. Karel was not even bothered by the stickiness of his fingers. There had been twenty oranges in the plastic sack and he felt he could eat them all.

'I like oranges,' Karel said. 'Nina likes the way I eat my oranges. She says it's like art.'

'Does she know how many you can eat though? Does she have any idea of the smell? And speak Russian for the grace of God!'

'She's normal. She likes the smell of oranges.' Karel said in Russian.

'She says that now, but believe me –'

'Can you just be quiet and let me eat my oranges?' Karel said and looked the other way. There was half of the orange left. He could not even think about eating it. It would dry up there, pucker in the summer evening's breeze.

Eugene tapped a cigarette against the wall, went to the window and opened the sash as he'd agreed he now would.

'What's going on outside?' Karel asked.

'There are a few lights on. The man with the baby's there. Jigging him up and down.'

'He's too rough with that boy,' Karel said. 'Every night too rough.'

'The child's got wind. Even I can see that.'

'He's too rough with him.'

'Since when did you think that?'

'I've always thought that.'

Outside an *ocabasi* a woman with tightly pulled-back hair was smoking a cigarette. She took a phone from her handbag and pressed a button. Karel's phone rang. He answered it, licking his fingers. Eugene watched the woman talk. He heard her talk into Karel's ear. He heard the frustration in Karel's English. His manic corrections. He heard him say no three times; say no three ways. He watched the woman walk away.

'She's a beautiful girl, your Nina,' he said. 'But the most beautiful women are from Minsk.'

'I never saw any of them,' Karel said. 'They must have all moved away when I lived there.'

Karel had a laptop and when Eugene was in they watched American cop shows, Russian soap operas, British football. It was a nothing match that night, but they sat on their beds, the laptop propped up on an orange crate and drank a few bottles of Budweiser. At the end of the game, Karel made a phone call. Eugene heard apology and anger in his voice. Karel ended the call and ate the last of the orange.

'Trouble in paradise?' Eugene said.

'I'm going to bed,' Karel said. 'A long day tomorrow.'

'Every day is long,' Eugene said.

'Watch something on the laptop if you want, I don't mind. But I must sleep.'

'It's not even eleven yet.'

'I know, Gen. I know.'

* * *

Karel sat at the card table peeling an orange. His hands were large and powerful, his fingers nimble and dextrous. By the time he'd finished, the flesh of the orange was scuffed with pith and odd spots of rind. He left it in the middle of his plate.

'Were you always in love with my mother?' Karel said. It was a Saturday and so there was vodka. Eugene was looking out of the window, the man and child nowhere to be seen.

'Did she ever talk of me?' Eugene asked.

'She said that you were kind.'

'Ah!' he said. 'Well you know what that means.'

Karel took a sip of his vodka and his phone wriggled in his pocket. The third text that evening.

'You could have been my father, I suppose.'

Eugene wanted to strike him. To get up from the bed and cuff the boy around the ear for his insolence. So stupid a reaction; this man the size of a bear, arm muscles to make boxers seem girlish. It passed in a shot of vodka and a pull of beer.

'I wouldn't have made much of a father,' Eugene said and sat down at the card table. 'You were lucky there. Your mother was lucky too.'

It had changed nothing: the story, the confession. And there was little to say in any case. Men who wander fall in love easily; Karel's mother was just the first and therefore most perfect of memories. That was the crux of what he had been explaining; but this had not been the lesson taken.

'I understand what you mean,' Karel had said. 'And thank you – that mustn't have been easy.'

They sat at the table together and Karel's phone eventually rang.

'I must take that,' he said.

'Yes,' Eugene said. 'Of course you must.'

* * *

Eugene plotted his route again on the small map, though he already knew exactly where he was heading, how long it would take and where to get off the bus. Karel's laptop was useful now he knew how to use it. He had used GoogleEarth and had seen the road on which Karel lived. There were no shops, no flats running like a mezzanine above them; just blocks and blocks of flats, trees outside on the pavement, cars double parked in white-lined bays.

Despite the planning, Eugene was a half hour early. There was a bar around the corner and he had an expensive bottle of Budweiser while a large crowd watched rugby. He ordered vodka and the bar staff, as accented as him but better dressed, served him his drink with suspicion. Their customers were eating roast dinners, drinking wine and beers and Bloody Marys. The pitch of the referee's whistle on the television cut through the loudness of their voices. Some of them looked at him. He downed his drink and quickly left.

There were forty-seven buzzers outside Karel's block. He pressed number 22 and Karel answered as quickly as eating an orange. At the top of the stairs he saw a long corridor with a single open door. Karel appeared, bigger if that was even possible, wide smile on a wide mouth, wiping his hands on a dish cloth.

'Gen!' he called out down the corridor. 'So good to see you!'

'Speak Russian,' Eugene said. 'It's Sunday, don't you know to speak Russian on a Sunday?'

'Come on in, Gen,' he said after they had embraced. 'Come see my new place.'

The flat was ferociously tidy, three rooms – kitchen/living room, bedroom, bathroom – with laminate flooring and the cheapest kind of furniture. There were two bowls of nuts on the coffee table and the small dining table was set for three. Nina was stirring a large pot on the stove. She looked like she had been stirring the pot for a hundred years.

'I brought some things for you,' Eugene said and took out some beers from his shoulder bag.

'Thanks,' Nina said. 'Good to see you, Gen.' She kissed him on the cheeks.

'You're looking well,' he said. 'It must agree with you.'

She nodded and Karel put his arms around her. He was big enough to envelope the whole apartment. She pushed him away and went back to stirring the pot.

'We have a balcony too,' Karel said and opened the fridge, poured beer for them both. 'Let's go outside, yes?'

They opened the door onto the smallest balcony Eugene had ever seen. It was just about big enough for them to stand side by side. There was an ashtray set on a very small wooden card table.

'So how are you?' Karel asked.

'Fine. You?'

'Fine,' he said. 'Excited, you know?'

'You have a lot to be excited about.'

Eugene smoked a cigarette and they both drank their beer and both agreed how good it was to see each other at last. Then Nina called Karel inside to help with serving lunch.

Nina was a fine cook and Eugene had three helpings of stew. 'You can come any time, Gen,' she said.

'Thank you, Nina,' he said. 'I shall hold you to that.'

After the two men had cleared the plates, they went outside again. The wind had got up and there were teeth in it. They agreed the food was good, that Nina was a fine cook.

'I have something for you,' Eugene said as they went back inside. Out of his shoulder bag he took a plastic sack and handed it to Eugene.

'Here,' he said. 'I thought you must be missing them.'

'Thanks, Gen,' he said. 'Look, Nina, Gen has brought us oranges!'

'Oranges?'

'Yes, look, from the shop I used to live above. Best oranges I ever tasted.'

'They were nice, yes,' she said and motioned everyone back to the table.

Karel sat at the table peeling an orange. His hands were large and powerful, his fingers nimble and dextrous. By the time he'd finished, the flesh of the orange was clean, pithless and perfectly round. He passed the plate with the orange to Nina. Just as he had, she split open the orange and quickly ate. He peeled another, split it, began to quickly eat. Eugene watched the two of them, the juice on their chins, the way they licked the juice from their fingers. He watched them smile and with his right hand, Eugene took an orange from the plastic sack. He dug his thumbnail into its flesh and began to peel.

POETRY

HANNAH LOWE

My Father's Butterflies

Looked more like birds, I thought; made of paper,
tightly folded, edge to point to corner.
His fingers gently worked the lines and creases
so the wings would beat upon their axes
and the butterfly have life. I took
my bristle brush and ink and dabbed the look
I wanted on each one – ruby splashes,
careful petals, polka-dots, black dashes
on their backs – so they belonged to me.
In his palms, the painted paper body
rested like a pair of playing cards,
perhaps the ten of hearts and six of spades,
what faced me when he cut a deck in two
and told me: *blow on the butterfly!* And I blew.

INTERVIEW

FROM READER TO READER

Sarah Coley talks to Frances Macmillan

Frances Macmillan is the Senior Editor of Vintage Classics at Random House and a good friend of *The Reader.*

Is it hard to get a job in publishing? How did you get into it?

I went to Vintage to do two weeks work experience in September 2006, to cover for the Publishing Director's assistant who was on holiday. Then I hung around for a week or so more and I was very lucky. A senior editor left and the Publishing Director gave everyone a promotion and offered me the now vacant job as her assistant. Work experience is the route I would recommend to anyone seeking a job in publishing. It gives you a genuine chance.

In a way that's like reading a new book, you know, how you invest in the characters and their lives, and you don't know if it's going to pay off or if anything will come of that first unrewarded effort.

Yes, exactly. You don't get a feeling for the person from the CV but working alongside each other – and we work together very closely at Vintage – you learn a lot about people, how we each express ourselves.

Is the atmosphere bookish or are you aware more of the business aspect?

There has to be a mixture of both. As much as we are all there as readers, publishing is a business, and in the case of Random

House, the umbrella company, a big business. It's no use telling an acquisitions meeting how a book moved you, or how beautifully it is written unless you can also say who it's written for and what other books like it have sold well. What will make this book stand out from the 1000 other books published each year? The book's effect might be intangible but the hard details count.

As a paperback editor, you read submissions alongside a hardback editor to give them the mass-market view. Even if the book itself is not your cup of tea you should be thinking about the potential audience and how it could be published.

My job now is very different in most ways. When I started I did mainly administrative work – always a big part of the job – but I was able to learn the ropes and even got to look after my own charity project and a paperback original or two. Then they started a Classics list, I got promoted, started looking after a few more titles and assisting the Classics editorial director, which I loved. Now I'm running that classics list myself, though I've only just got started!

What books do you draw from in making up the Classics list?

Vintage always had a big 'backlist', meaning they had published the works of authors such as Graham Greene, Aldous Huxley, Remarque, Pasternak, Somerset Maugham, Virginia Woolf, for many years. That's the basic list that the Classics list is built on. But in 2007, Vintage started publishing out-of-copyright works too – Dickens, George Eliot, and so on. If you take the case of Virginia Woolf – Hogarth was her first publisher, and that became Chatto, which was bought by Random House and became part of our heritage. Vintage started up in 1990, and when it did so it began publishing the paperbacks of all those authors who had been first published by now-Random House imprints (Jonathan Cape, Chatto & Windus, Bodley Head). The archives of Random House, in Northamptonshire, are an amazing place. So many different publishers came together over the years to form Random House, and that is quite a treasure trove to choose from when making your classics schedule.

How do you do go about whittling down this treasure trove to a manageable (and marketable) list?

FRANCES MACMILLAN

There's a lot of reading – titles such as *The Constant Nymph* by Margaret Kennedy, a book everyone read at some point but now we have all forgotten it. We have to decide whether to publish it as a Classic and bring it to everyone's attention again. We also publish lots of 'classic' crime (whodunnits) and books with a kind of nostalgic charm, writers of their time, such as Nevil Shute, Hammond Innes. Once upon a time those books had huge readerships and, packaged as a tried and tested 'classic' of its genre, they can find that readership again. That's at the other end of the scale from publishing a new translation of *Thérèse Raquin* of course, and we do that too.

Do you include footnotes and scholarly apparatus with a 'new' classic?

When they launched the new Vintage Classics list there was an important stage of consumer research, approaching different kinds of reader with questions about existing editions of the classics. This found that many people were scared off by an academic introduction or by forty pages of notes; people who would read a new bestseller but might not choose *Madame Bovary*. So in our editions we have introductions from others writers – they're friendly recommendations rather than rigorous explanations of the book.

So people want the text itself, the story, just as if it were a modern book.

Yes, when Vintage Classics started, there weren't many other publishers doing affordable paperback editions of classics. We put ours out with modern-looking covers, approachable intro-ductions, collectable design. That made us pretty successful at first, but competition has got stiffer since. And now you can buy *Jane Eyre* or the complete *Barchester Chronicles* for between 0–99p on Kindle, so we need other things to recommend our editions.

I love my Kindle. It takes up no more shelf space than its width no matter how fat I fill it. And I really like not having to return a book to the shelf.

I do too, I read the *Barchester Chronicles* by Trollope recently on Kindle and those six fat books were always with me. It would have been impossible to carry around so many physical books.

But, I have to say, since finishing, I really want to have those books as physical objects... I loved them and I can't expend my love on a computer file. It's that physical sense, books as *friends*; books that furnish a room; books to *give* to a friend as a brilliant present that we have to think about in our publishing now.

Tell me more about the readers. We're talking about saving books from the past but it's the unfathomable thing in a reader that is the life of a book. How do you find them? How do they find you?

The readers are pretty mysterious. It's like hunting down a mysterious animal using tracks and signs to work out their habits. We have a consumer research dept, and we have Twitter, Facebook, and all kinds of social media now. In that way we have more contact than ever but still, you're right, that deep connection is the lifeblood of a book and its impossible to engender or fabricate. It's a rare thing that we have to capture in order to survive. Our website is important.

Your website is really rather good. I was mooching through it and it's open, helpful, on the level.

Oh good! We're redoing it actually. There is a huge focus now on 'the people'. We have to talk endlessly, feed information, but not in a MARKETING BRAND / FOCUS / BILLBOARD ADVERT way. Like many other companies and businesses, the various imprints have had to find a human voice and a way to talk to their readers.

*What happened with **Stoner**? I remember back in 1999 John McGahern wrote a brief recommendation in the magazine for **Stoner**. At that stage, no one here had read the book, and now it seems everyone everywhere has read it…*

It goes back to what I was saying about not being able to fabricate that readerly connection. *Stoner* by John Williams has been around for years, since 1965. Vintage published it first in 2003. Somehow, reader by reader, word got about and it became a best seller in Europe, in France, Holland, Israel, Italy. People read it, got a surprise – here's something GOOD – and felt the urge to pass it on. Like a gift. We told people about it on Twitter, Here's a surprise best seller, have you read it yet? John McGahern wrote the introduction for our edition and he concluded:

> **If the novel can be said to have one central idea, it is surely that of love, the many forms love takes and all the forces that oppose it: 'It [love] was a passion neither of the mind nor of the heart, it was a force that comprehended them both, as if they were but the matter of love, its specific substance.'**

Love is both solid, it has a 'specific substance', and hard to grasp, a 'force'. Everyone who reads *Stoner* seems to find something honest in it and that is something unmarketable. It certainly took us by surprise. It was *not* the result of a marketing strategy! We were reprinting this backlist title week on week on week, 1000 copies, with no idea where the demand was coming from and that excitement went back and forth, from reader to reader.

*I guess people knew – like being at the theatre or a concert – that they were part of something that was happening. Books are slow. This was quick and alive, a genuine phenomenon. Does it put pressure on you to try to rediscover 'the next **Stoner**'?*

I'm trying to avoid talking about every new reissue as 'the new Stoner'!

*So what is the new **Stoner**, eh?*

I wish everyone would read Anthony Trollope – high time for another lavish BBC adaptation of the *Barchester Chronicles*! I loved reading those books because they are wise and funny and so generous, full of characters muddling along and trying to do the right thing.

POETRY

JONATHAN EDWARDS

The Hippo

       is solo, hobo, incognito,
two boulders curving out of Dettol-murk,
in a zoo his photo advertises,
doing a sponsored sitting-still all day.
Stop being a cliché, hippo, or I won't

write a poem about you. Then you'll be sorry.
What is your body but the verb *To wallow*?
What is the water but a part of self?
Google says you can crush a Ford Sierra
between your jaws. They don't say how they test this.

Candyfloss-high boys crowd your glass, betting
they could hold their breath underwater longer,
they could leap from one boulder to the other.
I abandon you
for the giraffes, stupid as window cleaners,

the lions, sunshine with teeth,
but keep coming back:
if you were to rise, show your eyes, your mouth,
would you have Martin Sheen's bandana'd head,
breaking smoke-water in *Apocalypse Now?*

Closing time. One last go. O please, hippo,
don't be so self-effacing, so tight-fisted.
Come on out, don't you know
we love you? Wait. Is that a flash of flesh,
a hippo peepshow, or are you still snoozing?

A little girl says, *Dad, that island's moving.*

ESSAY

BUZZ

Malcolm Bennett

I'm waiting for the bees.

Last time we had some delivered, they came by courier. Five wooden frames each holding a wax comb of hexagonal cells filled with honey and grubs, tended by ten thousand bees, and all sealed in a ventilated plastic box about the size of a desktop PC. The courier parked his van on the road and knocked at the front door, holding the box, nonchalantly, under his arm. I wasn't at home so Julie answered: 'Wonderful,' she said, 'our bees!'

'Yes,' smiled the courier, looking at the *Fragile – Bees – Handle with care* labels. 'What's in the box?'

'Bees. Can you hear them?'

Horrified, not just at hearing for the first time but feeling his cargo's hum, he dropped the box and, grabbing the signed delivery sheet, scurried back to his van. The understandably annoyed bees were still grumbling, their box vibrating, when I got home. This time they are coming by post rather than courier. Our posties (one does the letters and the other the parcels) are friendly and forewarned, so all should be fine.

We're getting more bees because ours died over the winter. I'm not sure why. It was probably a combination of things. It was a lousy summer and the colony didn't grow – bees don't like cold or rain so they didn't get out much and their honey stores were low. I fed them sugar water over the summer and fondant throughout the winter but they still didn't eat enough, perhaps because it was so cold and there weren't enough bees to cluster together and keep warm.

> **Flightless now and shivering,**
> **around the Queen they cling;**
> **every bee a gift of heat;**
> **she will not freeze**
> **within the winter cluster of the bees.**
> (Carol Ann Duffy, 'The Bee Carol')

In the spring all I had was a bunch-of-grapes-sized tear-drop of dead bees. This time we're going to do it differently. We'll bring the bees down to the house in the winter, as we have in earlier years, where it's warmer and less exposed.

We've never taken much honey from our hives, preferring to leave the bulk of it for the bees. Each worker bee in its lifetime of perhaps only six weeks produces just a drop of honey and each pound involves over fifty thousand bee miles, so I feel they deserve it more than me. Our new bees will be Buckfast bees, named after the Abbey where they were bred in the first half of the last century by Brother Adam. Of course, nothing can beat the honey we do take from our own hives. I love the way it changes through the year: clear and runny from spring flowers and apple blossom, dark and treacly from nearby woodland oaks and beech, hard and white from more distant oil seed rape. Rather, the joy of bees comes simply from their being there. 'Some have said that bees possess a share of divine mind, and draw the breath of heaven', wrote Virgil. There's definitely something Zen-like to be found in watching bees go about their work, observing their comings and goings at the entrance to the hive. The incoming worker bees have heavy pollen sacs in yellow, white, green or dark blue-black, depending on the season's flowers. In late summer they often have a Mohican of white pollen from the Indian balsam that grows along streams and whose anthers, through millennia of evolutionary engineering, are designed to slam down on the bees' heads as they sip from nectar pools deep in the helmet-like flowers. The sentries at the hive's entrance surveil these incoming bees, cheerfully checking bona fides, a quick antennal frisk, before waving their sisters in. But not would-be robber bees from other hives and definitely not raiding wasps, who if they persist will be set upon by a curling frenzy of guard bees ending in a tumbling ball of stinging death. The lazy drones (not too many), larger than their hard-working sisters and with out-sized eyes, float in and out, languidly courtier-like, their fates either terminal passion with a virgin queen or, ageing and pointless, to be cast out as autumn frosts arrive. And younger worker bees, taking time from tending the queen and their sibling larvae, form a cloud of wing-stretching youthful exuberance at the front of the hive whenever the sun shines hot, practising for when they are old enough to go foraging.

When all is well, a quick few minutes' check of the hive can easily become an hour's contemplation. When all is not well, this contemplation takes on a different, uneasy, texture. Superficially, the hive may look the same but it is not. Perhaps the queen has died, or some of the colony has swarmed, taking the queen with them.

The bees circle around a queen-less hive in the hot beams of the midday sun as gaily as around the living hives; from a distance it smells of honey like the others, and bees fly in and out in the same way. But one has only to observe that hive to realise that there is no longer any life in it. The bees do not fly in the same way, the smell and the sound that meet the beekeeper are not the same. To the beekeeper's tap on the wall of the sick hive, instead of the former instant unanimous humming of tens of thousands of bees with their abdomens threateningly compressed, and producing by the rapid vibration of their wings an aerial living sound, the only reply is a disconnected buzzing from different parts of the deserted hive. From the alighting board, instead of the former spirituous fragrant smell of honey and venom, and the warm whiffs of crowded life, comes

an odour of emptiness and decay mingling with the smell of honey. There are no longer sentinels sounding the alarm with their abdomens raised, and ready to die in defence of the hive.

(Tolstoy, *War and Peace*)

This contemplation of the hive has little in common with people-watching, or bird-watching or any other observational natural history. Nor has it anything to do with social commentary despite the historical and literary use of bee behaviour as a metaphor, or even paradigm, for human society. It feels more like a conversation, albeit silent, telepathic. It's easy to understand how the notion of 'telling the bees' about happenings in the family and village developed. It's particularly important to tell them about deaths, or, snubbed, they may leave.

**...and the chore-girl still
Sung to the bees stealing out and in.**

**And the song she was singing ever since
In my ear sounds on:—
"Stay at home, pretty bees, fly not hence!
Mistress Mary is dead and gone!"**
(John Greenleaf Whittier, 'Telling the Bees')

For it seems, as Rudyard Kipling put it, that 'the Bees are just about / As curious as a man.' This curiosity arises from the need to guard the colony, and bees dislike change. If you move your hive, it must be either less than three feet or more than three miles. Anything in-between, and the bees will return from foraging to where the hive entrance was, and hover, lost, until they die. Moving the hive from one end of the garden to the other can take weeks. The Roman agriculturist Columella wrote:

Very great care must be taken by the man in charge, who feeds the bees, when he must handle the hives, that the day before he has abstained from sexual relations and does not approach them when drunk and only

**after washing himself, and he abstains from all edibles
which have a strong flavour… from acrimonious stench
of garlic and onions and all other similar things.**

On the whole, our bees have not bothered people, or our cats,
although the dog sometimes has a rough time – whether this is a
matter of size or smell or both I have no idea. I once had a colony
of Slovakian bees that every month produced a single angry bee.
This bee did not like anyone, least of all me, coming near the hive,
and would chase me away. Indeed it would chase me down the
garden and seek me out amongst the runner beans: staying calm
and moving slowly did nothing to sooth this bee's temperament.
In the end, it was easier to let her sting me (or better still, one of
our sons) as that would be the end of it for another month – each
bee an unnecessary martyr to a non-existent cause.

Anyhow. There will be no honey for tea this year, as we're still
waiting for the bees.

JOHN WEDGWOOD CLARKE

Sleeping Child

You sleep, while names of villages rise
and fall away, taillights dwindling ahead
until only we summon the sign
for crossing deer, steer by the constellation
of a pub. The edges where the wipers
shove the rain gel and tremble, sucked thin
by small riptides. I rest my elbow on
the door-frame like my father would and read
the road through fingertips. A milestone
unfolds, lets go of the verge, the barn owl
gone before I realise. That's how we get home.
And what will you recall of the sudden lift
from car to bed, your eyes broken open
for a moment by the light in the hall?

ESSAY

JUST SHUT UP!

Philip Davis

Here is a proposition: It would be a better world were we less *literal*-minded and more *literary*-minded. If you were to ask me.

To which someone will retort: What *exactly* do you mean by *literary*-minded?

To which I reply: That is precisely a literal-minded question.

Literature is not about offering definitions or explanations or paraphrases: it is about showing you what it means, letting you feel what it means, creating an emotional human space in which you can test and try out what it means. Literature is about doing something – which also means reading is not just passive reception but is an active praxis: a craft that you learn how to do only by doing it, again and again, poem after poem, without it ever being wholly the same.

So I am going to try again to *show* something of what we mean by the quality of literary-mindedness by *doing* reading rather than talking about reading. What follows is a transcript of a reading group, but it is semi-fictionally adapted, anonymised, somewhat idealised and generally tidied up for these purposes as a result of interviewing a Reader Organisation project worker and reading her recording of two separate sessions on a relatively simple little poem by Thomas Dekker. The project worker chose this lyric because she wanted two quite different groups to think about the world of work and what it might mean. I am not saying it is great but it is interesting and can stand as representative of what a reading group might look at together:

Art thou poor, yet hast thou golden slumbers?
 O sweet content!
Art thou rich, yet is thy mind perplex'd?
 O punishment!
Dost thou laugh to see how fools are vex'd
To add to golden numbers golden numbers?
 O sweet content! O sweet, O sweet content!
Work apace, apace, apace, apace;
Honest labour bears a lovely face;
Then hey nonny nonny – hey nonny nonny!

Canst drink the waters of the crispèd spring?
 O sweet content!
Swim'st thou in wealth, yet sink'st thou in thine own tears?
 O punishment!
Then he that patiently want's burden bears,
No burden bears, but is a king, a king!
 O sweet content! O sweet, O sweet content!
Work apace, apace, apace, apace;
Honest labour bears a lovely face;
Then hey nonny nonny – hey nonny nonny!

Here is one group making a start.

Participant A: *This is making me uncomfortable because it is just a rich person telling poor people to be happy – telling them how much better off the poor are. Honest labour bears a lovely face is the Victorian work ethic.*
Project Worker: *Well, actually it is written much earlier. Two hundred years earlier than the Victorians. Thomas Dekker: 1570–1632.*
Participant B: *But in those days it was only the wealthy who were given a proper education. Dekker must have been one of the richer ones.*
Participant A: *And 'Hey nonny nonny' is just careless of the poor – it is like a shrug, just go along with it.*

Let's pause here for a second – because I want to say that this is obviously a clever start but it is a bad start. Because really it isn't a start at all. An intelligent participant has not liked this poem, has been offended by what he takes to be its ideology, and has confined it to a category – the Protestant work ethic – and a category in politics and in history – capitalism and the Victorian period. This is emphatically not literary-minded. It is not reading the poem, it is prematurely *interpreting* the poem. I am not saying that this suspicious thought – that the poem is a condescending attempt to cheer up the poor – should never enter one's mind when reading. But here from the outset it is dominating the mind, the poem, the tone – it's just a rich person telling poor people they are happy; it's just a shrug, hey nonny nonny, just go along with it. Whenever we see the phrase 'it's just' or 'it's only' in our recordings and transcripts from reading groups, we know that this is someone not really reading but being reductive instead. Give the poem a chance; treat it first as a stranger rather than fit it too quickly into your familiar box of the opinionated. Let it be present now, not confined to history.

So what is the poor Project Worker to do if some clever person finds good reason to dismiss the poem out of hand, from the word go? The job of the Project Worker, the Reader-in-Residence, the group leader or conductor is to try to get us into the poem, first of all, and then work *through* it, not jumping to a pre-established opinion but staying loyal to the pace at which it unfolds. So here is another go:

Project Worker: *Let's think about the language of this simple-looking poem. I mean, for example, there's a lot of repetition, of modified repetition in it, isn't there.*
Participant C: *You mean 'sweet content, sweet content', 'punishment'?*
Project Worker: *Yes, lines 2 and 4 in each stanza, 2, 4, 12, 14 structuring the contrasts.*
Participant D: *And the last four lines of each stanza are the same.*
Participant B: *I hadn't noticed that. I mean, it seems as if the last three lines in each stanza are the same, but I had somehow taken 'O sweet content, O sweet, O sweet content' in 7 and 17 to be more connected in each case with the earlier part of the stanza, especially with lines 2 and 12, 'O sweet content' of course.*

What is happening here? The Project Worker has switched the level of attention to the way the poem is written. But that is not because she is more interested in *how* it is written rather than *what* it says. She is not trying to be more technical for the sake of being technical. She is trying instead to stop the language being too quickly translated into over-familiarity. And abruptly as a result there comes a surprise – Participant B suddenly sees that though indeed in literal terms the last four lines of each stanza are exactly the same, actually the first of the four always seems to refer more to what precedes than what follows. 'O sweet content! O sweet, O sweet content.' We don't yet know what this means or if it means much, but that is the point: the reader is now looking at the poem as a working piece of music, with unexpected movements and modulations, and not just a flat thing on the page. Let's go back to another moment that follows from this in our reconstructed discussion:

Participant B: *It's funny isn't it that you get this line 'O sweet content, O sweet, O sweet content' immediately followed by something that doesn't feel quite sweet or contented – 'Work apace, apace, apace, apace'*
Project Worker: *What does that line feel like, then?*
Participant C: *It feels somehow driven. You can't seem to get out of it. The work carries you along inside it.*
Participant A: *Yes. It would be different, we would feel better, if there are only three repetitions. It is the fourth one that makes you almost breathless.*

Suddenly this is what I mean by reading. You can see this is not merely literal but imaginative in its guess-like search for the less obvious and less visible felt meaning: the participants are not longer saying it is *just* this or *just* that, but it makes you feel almost this or somehow that. A different part of the mind is opening here as the various minds begin also to collaborate together in the room. These people emphatically have got into the poem, are inside it.

Participant D: *That repetition 'apace, apace, apace, apace' is different from an earlier one I didn't quite understand, you know. It is line 6 – how fools are vex'd/To add to golden numbers golden numbers?'*

Participant A: *The golden numbers must be gold coins.*
Participant B: *You add them on and you add them on, and it doesn't make much difference.*
Project Worker: *They are just piling up. Golden numbers not golden slumbers.*
Participant C: *It is good he makes them rhyme,*
Project Worker: *But now for sake of contrast.*

These people are now reading, helping each other, and helping the poem. It is itself real work.

In another group at about this sort of point, a relatively rich man, a successful middle-aged business man, said:

Participant R (half-laughing): *I know this feeling, personally, at night sometimes, the 'mind perplex'd' – though I'm well off. Sometimes I just can't sleep. It's not always anxiety, it can be the excitement. But the golden numbers keep going round and round in my mind, apace, apace…*

To which a young woman on a low fixed income said:

Participant P: *I am poor – but I can't sleep at night, insomnia. And not only because it's a struggle to get by. But there's my brother. He's got nothing and is going downhill. And I can't really help him. And sometimes I find myself thinking I don't even quite want to either. I know…*

This was not like a clever interpretation about Victorian apologies for poverty and the honest worker. It felt triggered, almost involuntary, the sort of personal thing that rarely gets said in public – especially in a group of apparent unequals, here contrasting experiences without simple conflict. The group suddenly seemed like a better world, a better little society.

At this point R was looking at P with surprise, with new eyes, reported the project worker, as if they might be somehow quite differently also the same. They both miss the modestly happy ideal the poem ostensibly offers. The project worker then said, or rather re-read lines 15 and 16:

Then he that patiently want's burden bears,
No burden bears, but is a king, a king!

If you are poor but can't sleep for worry of it, then you are doubly poor. But if somehow – somehow – you could make it so that you were not worried, were content, you would be rich despite everything, More securely so inside than someone working away successfully in the outside world. Look how the burden of want shifts across those lines. A need not met is a want, a lack and a bitter desire, but borne patiently it is not a burden, as patience comes in place of desire. To bear the burden eventually makes it hardly seem a burden at all. – If that is possible – is it? how can it be?

Participant S: *Perhaps there are three groups – the worried rich, the worried poor, and this other group who are more simple and natural and content. They are kings, kings – if you could grasp it, despite the conventional world – not socially but psychologically, kings.*
Project Worker: *Dekker doesn't actually seem interested in the easy fourth option – the happy rich.*
Participant T: *So maybe it isn't about being poor at all, but being busy?*
Participant P: *In what you're doing, without having to think.*
Participant S: *Without worrying what you get out of it.*

This is what we are after in Get Into Reading: a break-through into finding deeper meaning, however minute or transient.

In both groups, people had struggled at first to understand these dense lines 15–16 about burden-bearing. But that third category of people – the impoverished who worked to make themselves not feel deprived – was the hardest and most interesting transformation. It was a great moment, another break-through, when R said

Participant R: *I don't think I quite understood this or maybe believed it. I sometimes know more about the dissatisfaction of swimming in wealth yet still sometimes sinking in tears, as if it isn't worth it or there's something else. But I do know this is different from that other use of 'bears' in the poem – not in 15–16 but in 9 and 19 'Honest labour bears a lovely face'*

Noticing something, half-dumbly pointing to something – some pattern or change or contrast of meaning is important here.

Better far than clever articulacy. In both groups that was the line that the Project Worker told me she most wanted to direct attention towards. 'Honest labour bears a lovely face.' In a poem full of varying repetitions, it still bore repeating, she told me. She next said something similar to both groups:

Project Worker: *This is life at work. If you are doing a job or someone is working for you, isn't it sometimes true, 'Honest labour bears a lovely face'?*

Participant A: *Even while working apace, apace, apace, apace?*

Participant C: *Yes, the pace and the stress are what you feel on the inside. The face of the worker is what is seen not by him or her. You can't see your own face.*

Project Worker: *You can't see the effect on yourself in the midst of doing it.*

Participant B: *But when you'd read it out loud the poetic stress was on the word lovely: 'Honest labour has a lovely face'. And has that face without knowing it, just having it and being it.*

Participant C: *And that makes honest seem open-faced too, allowing itself to be seen.*

This speaks of unselfconscious work, doing good without one's seeing it.

In the other group, R said:

Participant R: *This is why work might be great; can be important for us.*

Project Worker: *And so that's why 'hey nonny nonny' is like happy nonsense – you don't have to look for meaning. It is carrying a carefree emotion, a singing that is almost wordless, like an invitation to be unhurt, accepting it all without cynicism, like a solution at the end of a maths sum. QED.*

That is to say: work might be great. It could be simply happy. Not being so content is not, after all, evidence against this ideal but is rather the need for it. And poetry bespeaks that need.

And from the first group Participant B said:

Participant B: *I love it that the line, 'apace, apace, apace, apace', is not simply going on before the line 'honest labour bears a lovely face' but the two lines are going on together, at different levels, in a sort of refrain.*

I am concluding that reading is itself that sort of active absorption, that sort of lovely human involvement in work. Work which is about nuance and not crudeness. About sharing in practice. About creating sudden little communities in which the boundaries between private and public are re-drawn because of a poem's resonance. That is what practice means here – not just practising regularly, but learning a human craft. And that is what quality means here – not simply doing something well, but disclosing a quality of human being.

And all that is instead of literalness: chat, opinion, argumentativeness, knowing in advance what you and others are going to say and think. I wish we could stop talking so routinely and predictably for a while: just shut up. I grant you that we have to keep the human conversation going; I know it is wrong to repress the normal flow of ordinary things. But people are best in life when they talk really about what they have known and felt and experienced: those moments when we find our place on which to stand are our real poems and I wish we all tried to make those moments more frequent. And if we thought more like novelists, say, we would remember human specifics better, and be subtler, be less easily literal, about the characters we meet and recall. It would make a better world.

POETRY

THE OLD POEM

Brian Nellist

Edmund Spenser (1552?–1599)
The Faerie Queene I–III (1590)

1.

A Gentle Knight was pricking on the plaine,
Y cladd in mightie armes and siluer shielde,
Wherein old dints of deepe wounds did remaine,
The cruell markes of many a bloudy fielde;
Yet armes till that time did he neuer wield:
His angry steede did chide his foming bitt,
As much disdayning to the curbe to yield:
Full iolly knight he seemd, and faire did sitt,
As one for knightly giusts and fierce encounters fit.

2.

But on his brest a bloudie Crosse he bore,
The deare remembrance of his dying Lord,
For whose sweete sake that glorious badge he wore,
And dead as liuing euer him ador'd:
Vpon his shield the like was also scor'd,
For soueraine hope, which in his helpe he had:
Right faithfull true he was in deede and word,
But of his cheere did seeme too solemne sad,
Yet nothing did he dread, but euer was ydrad.

ON *THE FAERIE QUEENE*
Book I, 'Of Holinesse', canto I, 1 and 2

What book altered your life? asks a placard in Waterstone's window to which the answer should be some sacred text because that's what they're there for. But *The Faerie Queene* altered the way I read. Allegory, I thought, was like *The Pilgrim's Progress*, mysterious on the surface but clear to reflection whereas Spenser prompted questions all the way through. Six books in which knights set forth on quests concerned with some human quality, Holiness, Temperance, Love, Friendship, and so on, makes it all seem crystal clear but look at these two opening stanzas of the whole vast work. The language seems strangely archaic like that of a traditional tale-teller but surely such a writer usually offers us more help? Where are we, what is this plain, who is this knight? The verse movement seems fast and the knight is 'pricking', spurring on his horse yet we are held back. The metre is rapid iambics (kerthump, kerthump, though melodious and varied) but the rhyme scheme with just three rhymes has a couplet at the end and another in the middle to give a pause. The last line is longer (six feet or beats, an alexandrine) so the stanza is sealed off as a unit. Momentum and halts compose the reading process. Yes, we think, here is the conventional knight in shining armour except that actually it's old and battered while the wearer of it is young, and untried. Is he the Knight of Holiness as the title of the book implies or is it that neither he nor we understand what that means? It's that mid-verse pause that makes the trouble. Why is his horse angry and why does he use those spurs when he can scarcely control the animal. Why does he only 'seem' full jolly? No wonder the second stanza starts with 'But', offering a very different knight, devout, aware of the Christian story in miniature, 'dead as living'. The 'bloudie Crosse' reminds us of the 'bloody fields' in stanza one. Hope, faith and adoration, the Pauline trinity, sustain the knight but why then does this jolly knight 'of his cheere… seeme too solemne sad', with that telling use of 'cheere'? Can it be that he doesn't entirely trust those qualities that should inspire him? 'Nothing did he dread'; despite being 'faithful true', is it his own strong arm he prefers to trust? This is not a remote fairyland but a recognisable country of human contradictions and unacknowledged tensions. Read on!

ESSAY

PIRATE RADIO

Martin Boston

Now that I am moving into my 60s, semi-retired and indulging ever more my passion for listening to music, I am aware that I can trace its influence on my life from my early years, through school, university, travel, jobs, friendships, relationships: every aspect of my life in fact. I have started to write this as a sort of retrospective diary, not for any particular audience but certainly for my daughters to read sometime, to paint a picture for them of what made me what they have known and what I am now.

Below are two extracts from the diary:

1. In the early 1960s, I was allowed to take the green valve radio from the kitchen to my room when we acquired a wireless GEC transistor radio to entertain mum and Margie downstairs. That acquisition coincided with my discovery of Radio Luxembourg, with its frustratingly inconsistent reception and its policy of only playing at most, I think, seventy-five percent of a song before fading it out. Bruno Brookes, Alan Freeman, Stuart Henry and more: whoever it was, it was a chance for me to tap into the enticing world of pop from my sheltered life in middle-class Jewish Pollokshields. No particular songs stand out from my Luxembourg listening but it led me neatly into the Pirate Radio era and the love of music and the wonderful obsessions which are still with me to this day.

It began in earnest as a result of applying my sketchy knowledge of physics to the challenge of enhancing radio reception in my bedroom. I bought twenty feet of bell wire, stuffed the bared end into the aerial socket in the back of the radio and draped the wire around the dado rail almost twice, using sellotape to attach it tenuously to the wall. It worked. Radio Caroline was discovered. I was able to listen late into the night. I loved listening to Johnnie Walker, his Percy Sledge 'Warm and Tender Love' segment every night and his rapport with couples on the Frinton cliffs kept me transfixed. I remember vividly when Walker received his copy of 'Matthew and Son' by Cat Stevens. He played the section 'And he's been working all day, all day all day,' over and over again, lifting the needle and returning it to the same point on the vinyl each time. Walker seemed to me to embody everything magical about that time: no boundaries to anything in this new culture, this way of life, that was emerging beyond our experience as teenagers in Glasgow. And then came Radio Scotland with perfect reception and a chance to hear the chart songs, the new releases and, best of all, the American charts. Oh, the American charts!

Uncle Arthur, my mother's brother, had bought me the best Bar Mitzvah present a young man could have – a reel-to-reel tape-recorder. Every Sunday afternoon at 4 o'clock, I would set up the microphone in front of the green valve radio and tape *Pick Of the Pops* with Alan Freeman, trying desperately to time the Play/ Record combination to hit the end of his introduction and again before he cut in before the end of the song. I would listen back to my stop-start recordings throughout the week, providing me with plenty of material for school conversations and a growing body of useless information that would feed me throughout my life.

It was a great day in our house in Titwood Road when my dad bought our first stereo from Boots. It had two speakers locked to the deck itself, which detached and were then separated as far as the leads would stretch for pure stereo sound. It lived in the lounge permanently, which freed up the radiogram to become part of the den that my brother and I created in what was once our shared bedroom. It was a wonderful addition to our domain and it allowed us to listen to 'our' music without interference or criticism from the parents. I was given *carte blanche* to turn the room into a proper den and boy did I do so. The main wall was soon covered in a grid of nails, 10 by 8, each inserted through the centre of a 45 single displaying the full range of my cutting edge taste, from 'Madman Running Through The Field' by Dantalion's Chariot to 'Catch You On The Rebop' by Spencer Davis Group via 'Just Dropped In To See What Condition My Condition Was In' by The First Edition.

I remember buying The Monkees' 'I'm A Believer' and listening through a whole Saturday afternoon then turning it over and doing the same with 'I'm Not Your Stepping Stone' for the evening. Hour after hour until I knew every note and every nuance. Singles had to be listened to in that way, the B side often being as important as the A side itself. 'I Can See For Miles' by The Who was another but I can't remember the B side, despite its having had exactly the same treatment as the others.

2. Throughout the winter of 1971 and well into the spring of 1972, Alan Ramsay, a rather eccentric friend from school and the son of the Glasgow City Assessor, who lived in a massive house round the corner in St Andrews Drive, spent all of his time, spare or otherwise, rebuilding Lenny Wolf's Triumph Herald Estate which I had bought for thirty quid.

I watched, held things, fended off complaints from the neighbour who had generously and naively allowed us to use his garage and driveway and traipsed round scrapyards with Alan as we picked up spares for our project. We/he finally got it roadworthy and 'safe' and for several months that summer I drove it around Glasgow and to and from University, hoping to impress women, and in particular Jane Cochrane who was in my English seminar. I did give her a lift home to Giffnock once. That's it. Oh, and I purchased a tank aerial from the *Exchange and Mart* which we fitted to the bonnet to allow me to pick up the beloved pirate stations at night. We failed to attach it securely, however, and the 7-foot mast leaned at a worrying and dangerous angle, probably posing a threat to other motorists and pedestrians. It had to be removed eventually, after I had been stopped by the police and warned unequivocally that if I did not take appropriate action immediately, I would be charged with dangerous driving.

I had offered to take a friend's possessions through to Edinburgh as she was moving into a student flat prior to starting University. I had the radio on in the car, volume high as I accompanied Nilsson on 'Without You' which seemed to have been at No 1 for ever. As I entered a roundabout on the outskirts of the city, the elderly man in front of me inexplicably slammed on his brakes and I ran straight into the back of his car. The front of the Triumph folded neatly into a vertical triangle of sorts and a calm silence reigned, broken only by Nilsson still singing his interminable lament. The car was a write-off but the police were not interested in charging me as the old fellow took responsibility and announced how sorry he was but he had a nervous disorder. To this day I cannot recall how Judith's stuff got to the flat or indeed how I got home. The car didn't even have a decent burial. I just abandoned it there with Nilsson still singing his heart out.

Alan Ramsay was my partner in another short-lived project, The Crossmyloof Ice Rink Disco. We were always intent on finding ways of making money and making ourselves irresistible to the opposite sex. We failed on both counts! This project counted on the fact that there was next to nothing for teenagers to do on a Friday night in Shawlands, near where we lived, and that the ice-rink on Titwood Rd closed early on a Friday evening. We somehow persuaded the manager to let us run a disco for two hours for three weeks. I have no recollection where we found the equipment, but we did, and I was able to buy a small number of new releases as well as augmenting the selection from my own collection. I recall playing 'Black Night' by Deep Purple and 'Paranoid' by Black Sabbath, and wondering why the dance floor never filled. By the third week we had broken even, and while not having the option to continue, we were able to retire from our enterprise with heads held high. At least that's how I like to remember it. How many did we attract to those three disco infernos? We reached double figures for the first two but the third didn't quite reach that many and we were summarily closed down by an impatient and ruthless ice rink manager. Strangely, there were no remonstrations from our fans, no petitions for our return and our sortie into the entertainment industry closed for ever.

FOUR HELPINGS OF HARDY

SECOND THOUGHTS

'WAITING BOTH' AND 'THE GARDEN SEAT'

Mike Irwin

Some of Hardy's best poems are barely a dozen lines in length. Many are not merely short, but slight, comprising very few words. Such works owe much to the author's control of small effects of sound, stress, pace and tone. The poem generates an internal voice which becomes an aspect of its meaning.

WAITING BOTH

A star looks down at me,
And says: 'Here I and you
Stand, each in our degree:
What do you mean to do, –
      Mean to do?'

I say: 'For all I know,
Wait, and let Time go by,
Till my change come,' – 'Just so,'
The star says: 'So mean I: –
      So mean I.'

He thought well enough of 'Waiting Both' to make it the opening work in *Human Shows*. It comprises fifty-three words, all but one monosyllabic; forty-seven consist of four letters or fewer. Yet Hardy contrives to give his brief stanzas weight. The tripping trimeters are slowed by reversals of stress and by chiming long vowels: me/each/degree/mean, know/go/so, say/wait/change, I/I/Time/by. Six of the eight full lines are split by a marked medial pause. Sense takes primacy over metre, and establishes the measured pace notionally appropriate to inter-galactic conversation.

The repetition at the close of each stanza is a crucial factor: Hardy separates the phrases concerned with a double helping of punctuation, a line-change, and a space. The deceleration demands from the reader second thoughts that can diffuse the original phrase into a multiplicity of implications. The second verse concludes, extraordinarily, with six long, distinct, stressed syllables. In terms of pace and emphasis the tiny poem opens and closes like a concertina.

Two words stand out, prosodically emphasised: 'stand' and 'wait'. They recall, of course, the last line of Milton's sonnet on his blindness. Beyond that lies the assertion of Job: 'All the days of my appointed time will I wait, till my change come'. Unobtrusively Hardy establishes a long lineage for his poem.

THE GARDEN SEAT

Its former green is blue and thin,
And its once firm legs sink in and in;
Soon it will break down unaware,
Soon it will break down unaware.

At night when reddest flowers are black
Those who once sat thereon come back;
Quite a row of them sitting there,
Quite a row of them sitting there.

With them the seat does not break down,
Nor winter freeze them, nor floods drown,
For they are as light as upper air,
They are as light as upper air!

'The Garden Seat', likewise, is largely monosyllabic, and employs repetition. The opening verse is literal: the seat, once a sturdy physical object, is decaying. This process is mimicked, aurally, in the contrast between the triple stress of 'once firm legs', and the feebleness of 'sink in and in'. The repeated 'Soon it will break down unaware' seems merely a common-sense conclusion.

But the second verse slips into a different dimension. Darkness extinguishes the red of the flowers. In this mysterious nocturnal medium the former sitters can return, their lost reality at one with the temporarily vanished colours. Here the repetition of the final line implies a shift of tone so delicate as almost to defy decoding. It suggests: 'This is mere whimsy – there are scores of these people, far beyond the capacity of the seat. I cannot picture this notion, I can only conceive it. But the conception is a pleasant one.'

The third verse drifts further towards pure abstraction. A syllable is dropped at the start of the final line, which has the further effect of shrinking 'they are' to 'they're'. Closing, as it does, with four short syllables, the line is scarcely more than delicate exhalation. That insubstantiality alludes simultaneously to the fancifulness of the poem itself, the non-existence of the departed sitters, yet their surviving reality in the imagination. Here is a hint of an antidote to the decay of the seat.

THOMAS HARDY

IN HIS GARDEN AT MAX GATE, DORCHESTER

OPTING FOR THE REAL?

'HE ABJURES LOVE'

Bernard O'Donoghue

HE ABJURES LOVE

At last I put off love,
   For twice ten years
The daysman of my thought,
   And hope, and doing;
Being ashamed thereof,
   And faint of fears
And desolations, wrought
   In his pursuing.

Since first in youthtime those
   Disquietings
That heart-enslavement brings
   To hale and hoary,
Became my housefellows,
   And, fool and blind,
I turned from kith and kind
   To give him glory.

I was as children be
   Who have no care;
I did not shrink or sigh,
   I did not sicken;
But lo, Love beckoned me,
   And I was bare,
And poor, and starved, and dry,
   And fever-stricken.

Too many times ablaze
    With fatuous fires,
    Enkindled by his wiles
        To new embraces,
Did I, by wilful ways
    And baseless ires,
    Return the anxious smiles
        Of friendly faces.

No more will now rate I
    The common rare,
The midnight drizzle dew,
    The gray hour golden,
The wind a yearning cry,
    The faulty fair,
Things dreamt, of comelier hue
    Than things beholden!...

– I speak as one who plumbs
    Life's dim profound,
One who at length can sound
    Clear views and certain.
But – after love what comes?
    A scene that lours,
A few sad vacant hours,
    And then, the Curtain.

Hardy's 'He Abjures Love' is the last poem in the section of *Time's Laughingstocks and Other Verses* (1909) headed 'More Love Lyrics'. This lyrical poem has been set to music a number of times, most famously by Gerald Finzi in 1949, and it has always been a favourite amongst Hardy enthusiasts, though it is not exactly in the self-lacerating elegiac vein most associated with Hardy nowadays.

At least not in the usual way. The first four stanzas describe how 'At last I put off love', ashamed of it and faint from the fears and desolation suffered in its pursuit. For twenty years, from 'youthtime' to 'hoary' age, the speaker was fever-stricken with love, too often 'ablaze / With fatuous fires', so that he wilfully and with 'baseless ires' repaid gracelessly the 'anxious smiles / Of friendly faces', turning 'from kith and kind'.

So, in the first of these final two stanzas, he is giving it all up – all the misconceptions of love that made him think miseries some kind of exaltation: think common things rare or the midnight drizzle the lyrical dews of dawn, or depressed gray hours something golden. Love made him prize imagined things higher than actual, visible realities. So he is opting for the real rather than the illusory and the romanticised.

But there is a dramatic twist in the last stanza. The poet suddenly recognises the absurdity of this sage and solemn resolve with its 'clear views and certain': he mocks himself *'as'* one who 'plumbs life's dim profound'. He is speaking, portentously, *like* someone who sees the profound depths of things, at a level deeper than love. But, once we have given up on love, what is left for us? A few hours of loneliness and then – the final Curtain. The poem is, after all, saying that love is the most positive thing we have, for all its folly and childishness. This is not an argument for realistic disenchantment but a poem in the tradition of Shelley's transcendent love lyrics: 'The desire of the moth for the star, / Of the night for the morrow, / The devotion to something afar / From the sphere of our sorrow'.

Of the later engagements with the poem, the most memorable comes in Virginia Woolf's first (and wonderful) novel, *The Voyage Out*. Woolf's use of the poem also takes a romantic interpretation. Selecting some volumes of poems to take on a trip – the kind of trip you find in novels by Jane Austen or E.M.Forster – Mr Hewet, the Shelleyan organiser, ponders Meredith and Donne before settling on Hardy, from whom he quotes the final stanza here as appropriate to the elderly Mrs Paley. The tragic and idealistic heroine, Rachel Vinrace, is left representing love on her own, later looking at the fragility of a great yellow butterfly, 'opening and closing its wings very slowly' and asking herself 'What is it to be in love?'

Given the invariable final outcome, in poem or novel, realism is not an attractive option. It is clear from the unconvincing determination and resolve of the 'I' in the poem that the 'he' who abjures love in its title is making a mistake.

HARDY'S SIMPLE PROFUNDITY
'DRUMMER HODGE'

Jane Thomas

DRUMMER HODGE

I
They throw in Drummer Hodge, to rest
  Uncoffined – just as found:
His landmark is a kopje-crest
  That breaks the veldt around;
And foreign constellations west
  Each night above his mound.

II
Young Hodge the Drummer never knew –
  Fresh from his Wessex home –
The meaning of the broad Karoo,
  The Bush, the dusty loam,
And why uprose to nightly view
  Strange stars amid the gloom.

III
Yet portion of that unknown plain
  Will Hodge for ever be;
His homely northern breast and brain
  Grow to some Southern tree,
And strange-eyed constellations reign
  His stars eternally.

Writing to Florence Henniker on 24th November, 1899, Hardy
dismissed 'the 'thought [...] embodie[d]' in 'Drummer Hodge'[1]
as a 'mere passing one of no profundity, but it happened to be
curiously apposite to the moment'.[2]   Yet 'Drummer Hodge',

with its regular iambics, alternating tetrameters and trimeters and ababab rhyme scheme, is as profound – perhaps even more so – as any of Hardy's apparently more 'weighty' poems. The 'thought' embodied here is appropriate not merely to the local and national moment of its composition, but to more momentous ethical, philosophical and theological speculations on war and peace, imperialism and territorial rights, home and exile, life and death, God and Nature, identity and dissolution, and the relationship of human beings to the earth beneath them and the stars above.

The poem functions by holding competing ideas in an uneasy tension that is reflected in its fine resolution. The opening line with its jarring juxtaposition of 'throw' and 'rest' suggests the hasty, almost brutal disposal of a dead soldier's body and the familiar tombstone epithet 'Rest in Peace', minus its consolatory qualifier. The repetition of Hodge's name in each successive stanza specialises the rural boy soldier, but his grave is 'landmark[ed]' not by a tombstone with its identifying *hic jacet*, but by an anonymous 'kopje crest'. Unconfined by a coffin, Hodge's particular body will contribute all the sooner to the vast and general energy of the natural and cosmic world: his 'Northern breast and brain' become a 'Southern tree', his wondering gaze transmuted to the 'strange-eyed constellations', whose own finite stores of energy will be expended in supernovas from which the carbon atoms for future organic and inorganic forms will originate. In each stanza, body, earth and stars are, like Wordsworth's Lucy, 'rolled round in earth's diurnal course' but, unlike Lucy, Hodge is buried not in his (Wessex) homeland but in the dusty loam of the African veldt.

If, as Robert Pogue Harrison contends, the grave 'domesticates the inhuman transcendence of space and marks human time off from the timelessness of the gods and the eternal returns of nature'[3] then this boy soldier in his unmarked grave is forever, as Hardy puts it in 'The Voice', 'dissolved to wan wistlessness'. Hodge's struggle to comprehend 'the meaning' of the 'foreign constellations' and 'the broad Karoo' implies the deeper moral question of war – especially wars of Empire – and the larger existential one of life and death and the existence of

God. Where Rupert Brook's dead soldier colonised 'a corner of a foreign field' ('The Soldier') for England, for all time, young Hodge's 'Englishness' is appropriated and transformed by the barren plateau on which he fell. He becomes not 'a pulse in the eternal mind' but a scattering of atoms lost and found in new forms of life. His death may, in some small way, contribute to the colonisation of the Transvaal by the British, but the vaster unknown territory of death itself can never be 'domesticated' by the human mind. Hodge's exile in a strange land becomes a metaphor for the exile of the human spirit in death. And yet, as Philip Larkin says, death is 'the solving emptiness', providing both the solution and the dissolution of all questions and divisions.[4] Fighting to dispossess the Boers of their land, diamonds and mineral rights, in death Wessex Hodge becomes an integral part of its 'dusty loam', part of 'Earth's diurnal round', and 'a portion of that unknown plain' to which all human life is eventually exiled.

Hardy claimed that a poet 'should express the emotion of all ages and the thought of his own'.[5] In its simple profundity, 'Drummer Hodge' speaks not only to its, and Hardy's, particular moment, it also spoke to Rupert Brook's and to our own.

1. See Hardy's 'The Going of the Battery'.

2. *Collected Letters of Thomas Hardy* eds Purdy R.L. and Michael Millgate, Vol 2 (1980), p.238. On 2nd November, just three weeks after the start of Second Anglo-Boer War, the 73 Battery, Royal Field Artillery had left Dorchester Barracks to join the British forces in the Transvaal. 'Drummer Hodge' was first published in *Literature* on 25th November 1899 under the title: 'The Dead Drummer'. The headnote to the poem read: 'One of the Drummers killed was a native of a village near Casterbridge [Dorchester]'.

3. Robert Pogue Harrison (2003), *The Domain of the Dead*, p.23.

4. Philip Larkin, 'Ambulances'.

5. Thomas Hardy, *The Life and Work of Thomas Hardy*, ed. Michael Millgate (1984), p.417.

WILLING SURRENDER

'AT CASTLE BOTEREL'

Josie Billington

AT CASTLE BOTEREL

As I drive to the junction of lane and highway,
  And the drizzle bedrenches the waggonette,
I look behind at the fading byway,
  And see on its slope, now glistening wet,
    Distinctly yet

Myself and a girlish form benighted
  In dry March weather. We climb the road
Beside a chaise. We had just alighted
  To ease the sturdy pony's load
    When he sighed and slowed.

What we did as we climbed, and what we talked of
  Matters not much, nor to what it led, –
Something that life will not be balked of
  Without rude reason till hope is dead,
    And feeling fled.

It filled but a minute. But was there ever
  A time of such quality, since or before,
In that hill's story? To one mind never,
  Though it has been climbed, foot-swift, foot-sore,
    By thousands more.

Primaeval rocks form the road's steep border,
   And much have they faced there, first and last,
Of the transitory in Earth's long order;
   But what they record in colour and cast
      Is – that we two passed.

And to me, though Time's unflinching rigour,
   In mindless rote, has ruled from sight
The substance now, one phantom figure
   Remains on the slope, as when that night
      Saw us alight.

I look and see it there, shrinking, shrinking,
   I look back at it amid the rain
For the very last time; for my sand is sinking,
   And I shall traverse old love's domain
      Never again.

'At Castle Boterel' memorialises Thomas Hardy's visit, soon after the death of his wife, Emma – from whom in life he had been long estranged – to the place, Boscastle, where he had first courted her forty-three years before. The opening stanza seems to presage the final relinquishing of past attachments – 'I look behind at the fading byway': but, in the turn to the second stanza, as the words, like the waggonette, go steadily forward, the emotion goes seamlessly back. The poem is neither a neatly elegiac farewell nor a mawkish clinging to the past: it is a willing return and surrender, against the grain of age, loss and leaving, to old feelings, still rapturously young. Hardy opens himself so completely to memory that just as he is in it, it is in him. The unique emotion of this poem, and of the whole 1912–13 sequence of which it is part, comes from the generous risk it takes of no longer knowing the distinction between now and then, 'I' and 'myself', memory and being, the willed form of poetry and the unwilled content of feeling. Take that tiny word of continuity and contradiction – 'yet': just for a second, like a held breath, it gathers into itself the poem's precarious balance between lasting and fading. At the same time, by closing the rhyme and stanza at mid-sentence, the word holds the poem at once open and together, giving form from inside the feeling. So, at the opening of 'The Voice':

> **Woman much missed, how you call to me, call to me,**
> **Saying that now you are not as you were**
> **When you had changed from the one who was all to me,**
> **But as at first, when our day was fair.**

– the voice that is heard and the voice of the poem are not distinguishable. And on the strength and momentum of that involuntary reciprocity, the woman herself swings into view: 'Let me view you, then,/ … Yes, as I knew you then,/Even to the original air-blue gown.' This is the past Hardy could not bear to revisit while Emma was alive and unloved because he could not bear to be unmoved by it. Now, the more Hardy makes himself vulnerable to what the past has to give, the more that same disregard for his own emotional safety is rewarded – turning, in 'At Castle Boterel', to a kind of reckless confidence, even bravado. 'It filled but a minute'. That tiny moment becomes both smaller and greater when its infinitesimal human fragility is set in relief against the immeasurably infinite scale of 'Earth's long order'. Hardy sees how this moment looks from the perspective of all else in existence and insists upon its subjective power because of, not in spite of, seeing it so. 'Is' – that biggest small word in the language, magnificently isolated at the opening of the final line of stanza 5 – belongs entirely and forever to 'we two', even as the verb to which this coupled subject finally belongs awaits at line-end: 'passed'.

Hardy called the 1912–13 sequence 'an expiation'. The word is misleading, not only because these poems do not purge guilt or grief so much as restore the original love, but also because, in so doing, they do not relieve his pain. Hardy cannot be grateful for that restoration since he truly feels with it the sorrow of Emma's death, and more utterly alone than ever in the present to which the close of each poem returns him.

Thus I: faltering forward,
Leaves around me falling,
Wind oozing thin through the thorn from norward,
And the woman calling.

('The Voice')

Here, as at the conclusion of 'At Castle Boterel', past, place, poem desert the figure who 'remains', and remains to go on 'shrinking...shrinking... sinking', with feeling and memory still inside and still hurting him. Perhaps it is because, for all their power, these poems were too redundantly belated to offer either consolation to the man or love to the woman who most needed them, that their feeling stays inside the reader too, resonantly unfinished – there and not there, lost and not so, over and over: 'Distinctly yet', 'Never again', 'And the woman calling.'

JEAN SPRACKLAND

Taking Down The Scaffolding

Two stuntmen on a forty-foot tower.
One loosens the couplers, unclips the pulleys,
feeds through a gap above his head
a pole long as the house, for his mate
to lower over the roof edge –
it catches and he rocks it clanging free.

An hour later, they're nearly done.
The ladders and decks are chucked and stashed,
the apprentice checks them off and stacks the trailer.
And now to the blue plastic sheeting which has
snapped and billowed through so many windy nights –
they roll it thunderously and drop it through.

They know the risks, how much they can subtract
without collapse. They work together,
checking the angles, testing and sharing the weight.
They sing and banter, though one slip
could kill them both. What love you need
to dismantle the structure you're standing on!

Taken from *Sleeping Keys* (Cape, 2013)

JEAN SPRACKLAND

THE RISE EXPERIENCE

BEING VULNERABLE

JEAN SPRACKLAND AT HMP LOW NEWTON

Charlie Darby-Villis

While the twenty-five women waited in HMP Low Newton's library and Learning Shop for the visiting RISE poet, Jean Sprackland, I went to collect her from the prison gate. Later Jean told me how from the very first she was conscious of the particularity and peculiarity of the prison: how the process of locking up her phone and then walking through multiple doors and gates – the rhythm of locking and unlocking – produced a feeling of powerlessness and of restricted choices, so that as soon as she entered the room she empathised with the audience.

And she was warmly received: there was complete attention to the poet's gentle reading and conversation. Jean read and spoke with the women of Low Newton for two-and-a-half hours, reading from all of her poetry collections, some new unpublished works and then from her beautiful memoir *Strands*. A prisoner commented: 'Her voice brings her poems alive, calm and soothing, yet dramatic and funny. I would love to hear more in the future.'

I asked Jean how she chose what to read at events. She explained she had made a set list before the visit but abandoned it as soon as she began to understand the particularities of the audience, and started instead to pick poems that the women responded to, going with the flow. They liked particularly the narrative poems. 'Tattoos for Mother's Day' is an evocative sketch about her son. The women were taken not only by the poem but by the explanation of the inspiration. ('I loved her poems mainly because she explained her thought processes. It was very insightful'.)

Jean told me afterwards how *intimate* the event was, not as in small but emotionally close. 'Tattoos for Mother's Day' and a second poem 'Holy' created a bond with the audience through a shared experience of motherhood. Jean felt acutely at the time that this audience wanted to engage with her as a *person* and not just as a poet, and that intuition was proved correct in the women's feedback, one describing Jean as 'brave' while another wrote: 'She is a very inspiring lady who was not afraid to talk frankly of her own experiences'.

The connection continued through humour, a highlight for many being Jean's hilarious reading of a new poem about falling in love with a parking meter. One commended her for 'embracing her individuality', while others puzzled over whether this was a genuine attraction. This let Jean open up a great discussion about the differences between the 'I' in her poems and herself, the notion of poetic personas being new to most of this audience.

When we talked after the event Jean spoke at length about the relaxed give-and-take which made a contrast to the more formal experience of a public event. There hadn't been the veneer of flattery and politeness that can flatten out responses. The women were much more demonstrative and she felt there was an unusual level of honesty in both responses and questions. One exchange particularly stood out for Jean. During a break she circulated amongst the prisoners and was able to have more relaxed conversation. One woman came up to talk about the poems she had enjoyed and one that she hated, a poem that she had almost a visceral response to. Jean was really pleased that this woman was able to talk to her about this emotional response: 'It was really great, really great, to have someone say "I hate it"'.

This was what the morning was like, an open, lively and honest exchange about poetry and writing, completely focused on the work and what it can reveal about life. Afterwards Jean told me that the whole experience had been very powerful, and that it had taken her some time to wind down from the event. Her final words: 'It was a privilege to be allowed into this space, and I'm drawn to do it again'.

* * *

Half a year later I sit with a group of eight women in the same prison library. Every Wednesday morning we meet together and share stories, novels and poems in The Reader way. This morning we've grappled hard with a Tobias Wolff short story but now we have a complete change of tack. I announce that we're going to read a new poem by Jean Sprackland, 'Taking Down the Scaffolding'. One or two of the group weren't around in October but those that were perk up, particularly when they hear that it is as yet unpublished, that we're a first audience.

Perhaps everyone is still in the story but after I read the poem first of all there are rather blank first impressions. Only one person has a strong reaction, and it's negative. 'This is s**t, I don't like it.' One of the women presses her more closely 'What do you mean?' The first woman is firm 'This is about death and I don't like it.' This surprises the others, but then one asks a question 'You knew someone, yeah?' and then there's the nod, 'Yes, a friend died, falling off some scaffold.' Once again I'm struck about how quickly a personal resonance is brought up by a poem, often in unexpected ways. And struck also by the skilful question of the group member who knew how to understand the strong response.

Voices now begin to speak up for the poem. 'It's very visual, it produces a vivid picture'. Someone asks 'What about the brilliant last line-and-a-half, 'What love you need / to dismantle the structure you're standing on!'? That changes the whole poem.'

The poem is reread, this time by the person who told Jean about her hate for a poem. After the first reading of 'Taking Down the Scaffolding' she was surprised by her ambivalence, but warms to it now as she rereads it and starts talking about the importance of working together: 'There is something that is admirable here – it's about trust.' Someone else wants to go further. 'The last lines show an exposed vulnerability, someone coping without scaffolding, without armour. It's about a relationship – but it shows how trust in a relationship makes you stronger but paradoxically vulnerable.'

Someone else: 'I like this but it's about divorce. The scaffolding comes off and you have to stand alone, subtracting love.'

The ideas are coming fast and furious now: No – it's about addiction, alcohol – getting rid of your crutches. Or is it children and parents? Is it about growing up? Is it after all about death?

Another voice brings the group back to basics. 'We are over complicating this. It's about two men, about scaffolding, and it's purely visual.' Does this mean she doesn't like it? 'No, I like it, I like the picture, it's good to admire the skill of the workers. It would be a good thing to watch.'

Others don't want to be grounded in the occasion of the poem, convinced it is more than this. People start referring back to Jean's other poems. 'I really admire her writing – I like the way she writes about unobvious topics, two people putting up scaffolding, or that other poem about seeing a mattress from a train window, and then brings so much out of them.'

This mention of another of Sprackland's poems opens up the discussion and people start talking about her visit. I'm struck by how well people know her poems and am touched by the familiarity of the women; they talk about 'Jean', not 'Sprackland' or 'the poet'. There is a sense of this being a conversation about someone they know, a friend.

THE READING REVOLUTION

TRAFFIC

Casi Dylan

**Never to allow gradually the traffic to smother
With noise and fog the flowering of the spirit.**
  – Stephen Spender,
    'I think continually of those who were truly great'

**That is not it at all,
  That is not what I meant, at all.**
  – T.S. Eliot, 'The love song of J Alfred Prufrock'

It's a bit of a departure for me, but next week I will be attending my first ever intensive yoga course. I have high hopes for the week but very creaky knees, so I'm planning on using the time to see if I can commit myself more seriously to the practice. The location is not as glamorous as you may be imagining: Anthea, my teacher, runs her classes from a converted basement in a Partick tenement, just off the river Clyde. For the most part where you are barely seems to matter: breath and pumping blood fill your senses during the class, the focus drawn in on your own body. But it's in the silence towards the end of a session – lying on your back in *shavasana*, eyes closed, palms up, clearing your mind – that's when it becomes difficult not to hear the driving traffic outside on Dumbarton Road. 'Come back, come back to core,' Anthea says. 'Know where you are, from finger tips to toes.'

Lately, blocking out the traffic is on my mind. Over the past few years of running shared-reading courses 'traffic' had taken on a particular meaning for me; west-coast railway, mainly, buses and cabs. It's been new people in new rooms engaging with a new practice. Shared reading going places. Over seven-hundred people have now done Read to Lead. But lately 'traffic' seems in me to have reached a new stage of meaning. Now it means diversion, all the stuff that gets in the way. That blur between you and the best you intend to be and do. It's true that as a facilitator you live and work with such divergences. In your preparation for a session, for example, you'll be tuning into the 'hot spots' in the literature that you'll be reading together, marking in the margin those bits that instinctively stand out to you; it's these places that inform your access points into the writing. The vocabulary that we use to describe this process on the courses has a solidity to it, it's tangible:

'What is it that you have a duty to bring out in this piece?'
'What is undeniable in the poem?'
'What is real here?'

And yet another reality impinges on this when you take the session into a group. It may be that Jenny, the Occupational Therapist who supports you on the ward, is off ill today and hasn't been able to set up the reading room. Or Michael has had to leave the session – he's had too much to drink, it's centre policy. Occasionally you'll face 'I'm afraid that there's a lockdown in the prison, you have to stay here for as long as it takes.' Or it could be that Rita didn't sleep well last night, isn't feeling herself. Traffic of this nature is inevitable; it's the stuff of life, which as a facilitator you're here to work with, both in the books you read and the people you read with. It is your responsibility to cater for these various realities that converge in the group, and to explore the possibility of the literature providing suitable ground for a meaningful meeting-point. Those solid bits in the writing will be your guide, but what emerges may well not be what you had expected or planned. As a facilitator, you prepare yourself to balance as you go.

But running deeper and more destructive than these external divergences are the shifts that can take place within you, in which 'balancing as you go' would be all well and good if only you could remember where you were going. It happens in shared-reading groups as it does in life: vital passages are overlooked, undeniables denied. It's scary how easy it can be to let essentials go. Much of the work of The Reader Organisation is concerned with creating and maintaining a space in the world for that which is essential in literature, and that which is essential in our relationships with others and ourselves. To build an organisational scaffolding that will allow for such a movement and growth is to know the unrelenting need to go 'back to core', as Anthea would have it. To remember the roots of the revolution, to know them in yourself. And it's in coming back to that core that the scale of the work still to be done is revealed. It reminds me of T.S. Eliot in 'East Coker' from *Four Quartets*, as he simultaneously asserts the inadequacy and necessity of what lies at the core of his poetry:

> **That was a way of putting it – not very satisfactory:**
> **A periphrastic study in a worn-out poetical fashion,**
> **Leaving one still with the intolerable wrestle**
> **With words and meanings. The poetry does not matter.**
> **It was not (to start again) what one had expected.**

The writing here strikes me as brave not only in its honesty but for its recreation from within itself. The boldness of that line – 'The poetry does not matter' – could kill off everything with its downbeat ending, and yet immediately the next line is another try in expression, another beginning. 'I am a poet' it seems to be saying, 'and this is what I have to work with.' The only way about it is to start again.

* * *

I met Anna in January of this year. My colleague Amanda and I had travelled to Antwerp to run a Read to Lead course for a team of librarians and educators in the city. It was a powerful course for many reasons: a combination of the participants' enthusiasm and energy; the fact that we were working to bridge English-speaking and Dutch-speaking culture; that it still felt very much like the new year, the first course of 2013. The change that I witnessed in Anna remains part of its power for me. She was a young, accomplished woman, a librarian, fluent in many languages. She had previously worked as a translator. During the first day of the course, in which we were all getting a feel for working between two languages – often falling into the gaps between them – Anna would immediately jump in to translate for us. It must have seemed to her the natural role to play in the group. And yet this impulse to explain and correct, coming even as it did out of a will to serve the group, left little space for shared exploration of the literature. We had to fight the connection between us and the poem becoming too literal: a little stumbling after all is a useful thing.

At the beginning of the second day we read a poem by William Stafford, 'Ask Me'. It was the first time that I saw Anna left without words.

> **Some time when the river is ice ask me**
> **mistakes I have made. Ask me whether**
> **what I have done is my life. Others**
> **have come in their slow way into**
> **my thought, and some have tried to help**
> **or to hurt: ask me what difference**
> **their strongest love or hate has made.**
>
> **I will listen to what you say.**
> **You and I can turn and look**
> **at the silent river and wait. We know**
> **the current is there, hidden; and there**
> **are comings and goings from miles away**
> **that hold the stillness exactly before us.**
> **What the river says, that is what I say.**

After the reading there was silence for what felt like a long time. Then one of the group members quietly asked: "'Current': what does this mean?' It is Anna who answers, her reply this time coming from her hands. She places her palms together, makes a waving movement that reminds me of a swimming fish. 'It's this. It's what lies beneath, driving the water. *Stroom.*' Pause. 'It reminds me of my step-daughter.' Pause. 'She has autism.' Her hands move again. 'This is what I see, in her.' The moment was beautiful in its instinctive acknowledgement of the deficiency of literal translation. The Dutch word comes to her with ease, but the meaning – the literary thinking – is here expressed in the movement of those hands, those charged pauses in which a deeper connection between poem and person is made. Anna was a different reader for the rest of the course. She's got it, I thought.

Four months later and we are re-commissioned by *Stad Antwerpen* to run a follow-on masterclass for the very same group. Our subject was to be 'Shared Reading with Speakers of English as a Second Language', the experience of which would inform their work with the large and growing population in Flanders learning to speak Dutch. It was a subject and a situation which demanded a real imaginative ability on our part and that of the group, crossing from one setting and language to another: the success of the session would rely on the centrality of the literary language that connected us. I began with a deliberately challenging poem by ee cummings, an attempt to re-affirm the ability of the model to hold serious meaning and attention, and to create for ourselves the opportunity to live the inarticulacy that was the subject of our session.

> **how many moments must (amazing each**
> **how many centuries) these more than eyes**
> **restroll and stroll some never deepening beach**
>
> **locked in foreverish time's tide at poise,**
>
> **love alone understands: only for whom**
> **i'll keep my trust until that tide shall turn;**
> **and from all selfsubtractingly hugely doom**
> **treasures of reeking innocence are born.**

It became clear that a retreat to articulacy had taken place in the months since our last visit. So that in response to the exasperation of one of the group members – 'I feel that I can't speak English any more!' – Anna's unhesitating response comes as an explanation of the poem. As it had on that first day of Read to Lead. 'It's about… You see?' Where had they gone, those expressive hands, those pauses, that responded so beautifully to 'Ask Me' in January? Their profound acknowledgement that: 'We know the current is there, hidden.' Because – as much as there will always be some need to explain or define words for one another – what can one do with 'foreverish' or 'selfsubtractingly' other than to respond from the poetic imagination which they demand?

I do not mean to suggest that the slip back from breakthrough here is exceptional, irreparable, or that the commitment to shared reading is anything other than heartfelt. This is part of the difficulty. Even those most committed or exposed to the shared reading movement can become distanced from the practice within themselves. This is the danger involved in building a profession, an organisation, that the work becomes perfected and separates from its function. To come back to T.S. Eliot:

> **There is, it seems to us,**
> **At best, only a limited value**
> **In the knowledge derived from experience.**
> **The knowledge imposes a pattern, and falsifies,**
> **For the pattern is new in every moment**
> **And every moment is a new and shocking**
> **Valuation of all we have been.**

It was all too easy, coming back together for such a seemingly targeted masterclass, to pigeonhole this element of practice, and to forget that necessary adaptations between the various needs and settings of groups do not move us away from what we learned at the beginning. The most important moment of that masterclass was when my colleague Helen – as if it has only just occurred to her, turning away from the flipchart with a pen in her hand – reminded the group: 'Remember, this is not a literacy project. It's reading for pleasure. Don't lose faith in the power of the literature.' That which is 'new and shocking', 'new in every moment' – the stuff that sometimes escapes articulation – is the return to core. Knowing yourself from finger-tips to toes. That with this comes the 'valuation of all we have been' is the bloody difficult bit. Difficult to keep on wrestling with words, to read for meaning, to need and depend on literature as much as we promote it beyond ourselves. But we are readers, and this is what we have to work with.

POETRY

BARNEY EDEN

Feel

You want to know how I feel?
You take a step into a dark passage
Some stone steps, a dim light
A dark door
And the sign says
'angels fear to tread'
Do you open the door?
Can you open the door?
I cannot open it
I am the door

THE READING REVOLUTION

TEN STORIES
PASTORALIA

Alexis McNay

'Will you freaking talk to me?' she says. 'This is important. Don't be a dick for once.'

I've never been called a 'rat' before, but I can't imagine being much happier about it in any other circumstance. My accuser sits across the table, all the points of his angular face, via the intensity of his eyes, converging on me as he flaps his arms about to emphasise his point like a rapper. Like an angry scouse rapper. I don't think he's really angry, though; he's making a show, and all the bluster and body language has been called up in defence of a deeply embedded ideal that has become beyond the need for thought or interrogation: you never *ever* rat on anyone, no matter what, *ever*. Never. He is made to dig in, because one or two of the other men in the group, myself included, are not so sure, and keep trying to flank him, 'well, yes... *but*'. He is not shifting, and probably never will, ever. Yet he is being made to fight a little – to *think* a little? – and it can't escape his or the other men's notice, the precariousness of any absolutely inflexible position when it has to resort to the authority of 'you just don't do it'. The argument might be a stalemate, but the battleground itself provides a little victory. It's why it's pleasing to see J's impassioned contortions. His position is informed by his sense of reality, by the codes learned in a life opposed to authority, where it's a crime to betray even an enemy to *the* enemy, and where you sort out any problems yourself. It's a code sharing the moral murkiness of *omertà*. It's his truth, though, and I respect that, although I don't think it would withstand a full frontal assault. Those contesting his position do so from one based on a much more relative reality; partly because it allows for the possibility that the truth is always a tricky negotiation, and partly because the reality of this idea comes out of a work of fiction. Here's why I don't mind so much being called a rat (although I don't think I am, let me say). J had wasted no time at the beginning of this session – his first – in letting me know that he doesn't read fiction, 'made-up stories', but prefers the evidential authority of 'true-life', factual stuff, like autobiography [don't get me started] and true-crime [!]. After all, what's the point in reading and thinking about things that haven't actually happened. I countered with a customary response that I peddle out on the frequent occasions when this view rears its head, but J is not easily swayed. Thankfully, I have brought George Saunders' short story 'Pastoralia', about a man whose job it is to be a live-in cave dweller in the prehistoric section of a history theme-park.

* * *

Anyone who has browsed the shelves of a prison library will have shuddered at the amount of crime fiction and 'true-crime' memoirs of ex- (either reformed, born again, or simply too old) criminals that are stocked, presumably to supply the demands of the readership (though the distinction between supplying and channelling demand is always problematic). One can understand the appeal, of course, in terms of common experience, identification and even, sadly, aspiration, but my conversations with prisoners such as J have suggested also, in the case of the material that claims to be factual, that it is sought to deliver some kind of truth. I've found this taste for 'true-life' literature very common both in prisons and in drug and alcohol rehab settings. The idea seems to be that there's more weight, authority and pleasure to these books; that the lessons they contain are worth listening to; that the vicarious pleasures they hold have an added frisson for having happened. I wonder whether also they betray in this demographic of troubled backgrounds and psyches a deep need for stability and an anchor to some kind of known. It worries me if this is the case, but of course it's reading, and it's a start, and we don't proscribe. At another prison shared-reading group, where we meet in the library, a man claims to be a 'big reader'. 'I'll show you the stuff I read', he says, wanting to please. I follow him, and with an expansive sweep of his arm he indicates the deathly confines of rows of serial-killer and criminal biographies. 'I've read *all* of these', he says proudly, pointing out a line of *Chopper* books. My heart sinks as I say 'Great!' and quiz him on the appeal. Whatever I think about the reader's quest for and belief in the 'truth' in these kinds of book, I think that it's perhaps even more damaging that there is a corresponding view that the truth cannot be found in fiction. It's made-up, after all, or, as one man actually put it, 'fiction is just lies'. For me, the converse is true. Philosophically speaking, you're closer to the truth with good fiction. Philosophically speaking, whether in prison or the world generally, if truth is confined to the manifest terrain of reality, then we're all in trouble. We need for it to include the realm of possibility. This, of course, is a work of the imagination.

As I've grown older, the sense of 'truth' as something I might get my hands on and definitively 'know' has receded. My default position is of uncertainty, a dizzying apprehension of the relativity of everything; yet I know truth when I see it, or rather when I *feel* it. I suppose I'm more certain of truth as a feeling than as a fact – something that speaks to the soul and reminds us that we are alive in more than just a material way. I sit here and listen to 'Better Get Hit in Your Soul' by Charlie Mingus, and every note played by every musician strikes me as the truth, in a way that much stuff that actually goes on in the world and can be empirically tested doesn't. 'Absolute occurrence is irrelevant', says Tim O'Brien, in *How to Tell a True War Story,* 'a thing may happen and be a total lie; another thing may not happen and be truer than the truth'.

As we begin reading 'Pastoralia', we are not exactly grounded in the truth; the story's scenario is definitely 'made up', the narrative tone playfully foregrounding the contrivance, but very quickly something takes hold in the room which seems very truthful in that more meaningful way. The first thing is uncertainty, for which we have the fiction to thank. Uncertainty is a very genuine, widespread and valuable truth, though you wouldn't necessarily know it walking and talking around prison, where, on the surface of things at least, most men, like J, are cock-sure of how things stand with the world and with themselves. Let's rattle that up a bit. There's uncertainty about how the narrator should behave when confronted with his dilemma, which leads to me being called a rat, but that's later. First, there's an uncertainty which I think could be expressed as 'How should I *feel* about this?' You feel it in the room, because the story is out of kilter with 'reality', because it's told in this clever but slightly goofy way, because it's funny ('Am I allowed to find this funny?') but suddenly surprises you with its seriousness. I am quite sure that nobody in the room has ever read anything quite like this, and the disorientation opens up the possibility of finding something. Reading something like this with a prison group, you might see more little glances exchanged between the men in the room. Some of these are open, giggly or scoffing, some more surreptitious, which seem to be about reading others' reactions as a gauge for their own. I like this, because it suggests that all those truths and knowns from the street or from prison have not equipped you for this story, and you need help from others. It seems at these moments that there is heightened focus on the story, that the openness and receptivity of the group is enhanced. The collective work of making sense of, the challenge to tried and tested responses, the sharing of humour, the generosity generated by emotion, the friction generated by thought – as I look around the room at these predominantly young lads, unused to this kind of thing, I suspect, gathered around as if for warmth, it seems that some primal need, some deep truth, is being served. Something is happening, unobtrusively, naturally, which is important, but which doesn't happen enough.

I need to quickly describe the central tension in 'Pastoralia', the one that creates the heat in our room (this description won't do; read the story, on your own if you must, but preferably with a combative group). The story's tension is generated between the narrator and the (cave) lady colleague with whom he cohabits. It is caused by difference in their attitudes to work; unable to countenance the absurdity they both feel, she frequently flouts their contractual requirement for Neanderthal verisimilitude by speaking English or doing the crossword, while he grunts his disapproval. But the real tension is caused by their similarities – they both desperately need their jobs, as both have family dependents that are stricken in one way or another. Add a job-threatening recession-based downturn in visitors (people 'poking their heads in'), a cynical daily peer-review form which encourages what J would call 'ratting', and you have a dilemma finely poised for tragedy, where both alternative right courses also do wrong; does he risk his job and lie about her performance to save her and her dependents, or tell the truth to save his and condemn her?

As we discuss this point – and we go on for about half an hour – lots of little truths come into view. They are perhaps not significant enough to be registered by the world at large, but here they are as *felt* by me and I hope by others in the room. I'm aware of different positions brought into sharp relief by the literature: there's J's intransigence, which might suggest the limits of fiction if he weren't arguing with sufficient force to suggest that it matters. On the other hand, and matching all J's physical contortions with their own mental wrigglings trying to reconcile the story's complexities, are a number of men who have taken it to heart. Here's why I think fiction delivers us the truth. Had I brought in a real-life story about two prisoners condemned to share a cell, bound by a code of silence, impotent against the array of forces conspiring against them, it would be unlikely to have been as well-written, as funny, or as *true* as Saunders' story. More importantly, by making obvious the terms of reference, it would have diminished the imaginative work done by many of this group of readers. The process of identification that did take place – and there were those that saw parallels with prison experience – seems more valuable because such referents were obscured; what seemed to be happening in some cases was a little leap of the imagination to think 'this is like me', and then a little leap back saying 'but it's different in this way'. The individual's stake in the universal. Now I'm no neuroscientist, but this is surely better use of the brain's empathy muscle. It doesn't happen so much with J; he remains resolutely 'I', exhibiting a solipsism which is quite common in prison in my experience, although much of this identity seems to me to be persona. He can't or won't make that imaginative leap into the life and mind of the character. He remains in the comfort zone of black and white – ratting is a no-no – while others explore the grey matter.

For some, the story appears to vex a deep class-based consciousness that sometimes it's hard to act on your political beliefs without going against the instinct to protect your nearest and dearest. They understand the urge for solidarity with a colleague, but, on the other hand, 'It's his family on the line', they say, '…his son…' A couple of men, unable to commit, say things about not knowing how they'd deal with that situation until they were in it. They don't seem to get any satisfaction from that admission, and it seems braver and truer for it. Another young man, M, seems genuinely piqued at being cornered when he says, 'I'd have to (*if I were him*' implied) just leave and take my chances'. It's a noble thought, at least wresting some pride, moral integrity and self-determination from the manipulations of the story's cynical corporate world. M would not 'rat', but nor would he remain to be judged or disciplined by his Orwellian employers (a debate, here; some think that if your trust in power has been undermined by double-speak and exploitation, then it's OK to share in its dishonesty. Others think that in dealing with a system with compromised values, it becomes more important to hold on to some enclave of truth). Anyway, M is reminded by some in the group that the narrator's desperation to hold on to his job – to be doing it in the first place – doesn't suggest that there's much opportunity elsewhere. Walking away still leaves the question of who pays for his son's medication.

Another man, reading not only the narrator's circumstances, but his personality, too, says, 'yes, but this man wouldn't have the guts to walk away'. It's been half an hour. 'It's just a story!', someone says. We move on. We've deliberated over a piece of fiction, we've arrived at no consensus that might be called truth. All we've done is congregate around a problem – doing the right thing – and find individual ways of being troubled by the lack of a satisfactory solution. But it's the soul that's been troubled, and the delving, the listening, the subtle shifting (in some cases), the imagining of ourselves outside of ourselves to confront a moral conundrum in an abstract world is a confirmation of the presence of that inner life needed to confront and weather the concrete problems of reality.

My favourite instance of a moment of truth arising out of fiction was with a very different group; five middle-aged ladies and myself in a library group in Birkenhead, reading *Jane Eyre*. When we finish reading the moving death of Helen Burns, stoical and content to the last, steeled by her faith, one of the ladies sits back, looking exhausted but vindicated. 'You see!', she declares, '…there is a God!' I couldn't agree with the conclusion, but I couldn't but be moved by her conviction, which was an emotional response to words on the page read out with feeling and shared. What had apparently confirmed her faith in God had been for me and others in the group a little confirmation of our faith in humanity. Fiction does much more than create a 'made-up' world to which we can escape; that imaginative act of 'make-believe', caring for and responding emotionally to characters – and, importantly, *language* – which echoes with what's most importantly truthful within us can reflect back, enriching the world to which we return. How important, this, in an environment such as prison? I see some of the implications between the lines of this testimony, written by JB, a long-standing Read and Relax group member who was present when we read 'Pastoralia';

I have always liked reading books but since I have been attending the read and relax group I have been reading books that I would not normally read. This has opened

my reading experience and I find that I can relate with some of the characters better now than I did before. This has also made me read between the lines more and I also found myself wondering what meaning the paragraphs have and sometimes going back over what I have read, which I would not have done before attending... this makes more of an enjoyable read.

There's nothing in here explicitly about the role of shared reading, but those great words – 'opened', 'relate', 'wondering' – all employed to describe changes to a personal reading experience, a spirit of engagement and enquiry with a more open stance not just to the literature, but between the self and the world, have all relied on what we do as a group.

An idealistic search for truth increasingly seems to demand a cynical suspicion of much of what is presented as and passes for 'fact'. As in the world of 'Pastoralia', so in ours; the perverse and pervasive logic of market forces and self-interest generate so much counter-intuitive bullshit, so much noise, that we can become mute in the face of it. If we submit to the truths presented by a consumer culture, then we risk that 'getting and spending, we lay waste our powers'. If we look elsewhere, we feed off crumbs. Truth with a tiny 't' stalks the prison landings, waits restive outside the prison gates, and often infiltrates the reading room; a conversation prompted by the face-off between materialist and more spiritualist philosophies in Jack London's *The Sea Wolf* degenerates before my eyes into a tawdry argument between two men about how much it's possible to earn selling crack on the streets of Anfield and Kensington. These half-hours, where we forget all that, or at least where the way we think, talk – argue, sometimes – and feel like true people, bring to the surface something more genuine than that. They are a hit for the soul.

He looked really shocked and didn't take it out the bag, as if he could hardly bear to see it. A bit later, turning away from me, he said, as if to himself, 'I'll never doubt anyone again...'

But he didn't put it on, just held it in the bag. I was puzzled by this reaction, as I'd have said he was a very impulsive boy. But there was a stillness, a holding back – he'd got something he'd dreamed of, and now was a bit worried. In the end I said to him, 'I'm worried it might be a bit small, it might not fit, we might have to cut the feet off it... do you want to try it on?'

'It's OK,' he said. 'I am small. It'll fit.' And he put it on, over his school uniform and it was rather small, and looked very funny when he put his school shoes on over the feet.

Luke is aged 9, very, very hyper, he literally can't sit still, never reads for more than two or three minutes, doesn't seem able to concentrate, and yet conversationally he is intelligent and witty. The feeling you get from him is that he is unsecured, he's banging around the universe, and he doesn't *want* to stand still and be in one place.

With some of the other boys there are similar types of behaviour but you feel the underlying difficulty is different. Nathan, for example, sometimes becomes a Komodo dragon and runs around the room on all fours, flicking his tongue, but it feels to me as if he is much less conscious of his predicament, and is acting freely and spontaneously. Luke's banging about feels deliberate, as if he daren't be still.

Luke's a good reader – in a previous session I'd noticed that he was the only boy who could read the word 'fierce' without any help. So the technical ability is there, but the ability to focus, to concentrate on something for any length of time – even minutes – is lacking.

Luke lives with his Nan, and mentions that from time to time, and has once mentioned he doesn't have a mum. I don't know any more about his family background than that.

As part of the Reader in Residence day we have a one-to-one reading session where we read to each other. The other boys react very positively to this one-to-one time, and often quickly develop the confidence and concentration they need to read a whole book, but Luke has always just played or chatted in these sessions, or if pressed read a tiny bit or listened a tiny bit, then he's up and walking around the library, changing the subject, looking for something else to do or play with. While I try to encourage him to stay concentrated I always want to let him set the agenda. So when he wanders off to the suitcase and says 'Shall we play Boggle?' I say OK. He's good at Boggle and sometimes beats me.

The Reading Club has this advantage over classroom time, that we have no syllabus to get through, and our motive is always aiming for pleasure. The tiger suit was simply to make him feel happy. I'm sure everyone knows that pleasure is a precursor to learning and indeed a sign of it. One has to be interested to make that electrical connection.

I don't know why, but on the day I brought the tiger suit, I thought I'm going to try that Anthony Horowitz graphic novel *Point Blank* today, and showed it to Luke and asked him if he wanted to give it a go... I thought the speed of the pictures might help him as he is so jumpy himself. 'Look,' I said, 'It's like a comic...' He said OK and we started reading together. He seemed willing to be interested but at the point where the drug dealers' Skoda is seen outside the school he absolutely froze. I felt his body change; he went onto alert. I suddenly thought, 'Oh no, his mother is a drug addict'. I don't know if that is true, or why I thought it, but it hit me strongly as a possibility, this is why he lives with his Nan, this is why he doesn't see Mum. I said to him – Are you OK, do you want to go on reading? He nodded, and said 'Yes', very quietly and with great seriousness.

We read on to the point where the prelude bit ends – after Alex has dropped the dealers into the Police Conference. It took about fifteen minutes – and that is the longest Luke has been still in the six months I've known him. He was almost rigid with concentrated attention. As it was a natural break in the story, and as I was worried about him, I said, 'That'll do for today won't it, shall we go on to something else?'

He agreed and we started looking at one of the other books. Luke seemed quiet, but OK, as if warming up back to his usual self. Later when the other boys arrived for the reading club, he, still in the tiger suit, made himself a spacious and high-walled den in a corner and covered himself with a blanket, looking awfully like a baby in a tiger babygro. When the other boys were all there I read to them from *Emil and The Detectives*, and he seemed to be listening from his den.

All the same I went home thinking 'Mistake! Mistake!' worried that I'd stumbled into dangerous territory... *If* his mother is a drug addict, *if* he doesn't see her for that reason... His stillness had been so remarkable; I couldn't get it out of my head. It was like seeing an animal sensing danger.

Next week he arrived for his one-to-one, and immediately put the tiger suit on like a man who always owned one, and I said to him 'What would you like to read this week?'

'That book we were reading last week.'

'Oh now, which one was that?' I ask him, because during the afternoon session of the club we always get through a lot of books, but I think he is talking about *Point Blank*, and open the book suitcase so he can pick it out.

'That one,' he says, picking out *Point Blank*. As we sat down to read, he asked if there were any more books by this author, and we looked on the library shelves and there were loads, and Luke collected them all and piled them up on the library table in a wall reminiscent of the wall he had built last week when he lay down in his den, and we looked at them one by one. I thought this was more of the old distraction behaviour but Luke looked at each one very carefully, and we spent some time on one that had pictures of all of Alex Rider's gadgets. Then, after a short while of comparing titles, Luke picked up *Point Blank* and said to me 'Come on, let's read it.'

We sat at the library table for 20 minutes and read it together, taking turns to read bits of dialogue. Luke was totally absorbed, utterly concentrated. Then his one-to-one time was up and I told him he would have to go back to class while Thomas had his one-to-one time. Luke begged and pleaded not to go back to class, promising to be good, but I said to him 'You won't be able to be good – you know what you're like! You'll talk! And Thomas needs his one-to-one time'. All very normal.

Luke said, 'I'll just go round there, round the corner, and read this... I'll be quiet, I promise.'

Although anyone who knows Luke would say this was impossible, and soon he'd be being sent back to class with his tiger tail between his legs, I let him stay in the library. I couldn't resist the idea that he would read *Point Blank* on his own. He went round the corner in his tiger suit and lay on the giant beanbag and read silently to himself.

Thomas came in, and we got going on *Wild Child* by Jeanne Willis. After about twenty-five minutes, Thomas said to me, 'Do you think Luke has fallen asleep?' and we peeped round the corner but he was just lying there reading. He had a few pages of *Point Blank* to go.

Later, during Reading Club, I heard him recommending *Point Blank* to another boy. 'I read a whole book today and it was a really good one, it's called *Point Blank* and it's got Alex Rider in it...'

I start reading *Emil and The Detectives*, and when I asked 'Who remembers why Emil had money in his pocket?', it was Luke who shouted out. He remembered everything – as he lay there the previous week under the blanket in his tiger den he had been listening to every detail. He had been concentrating.

Today, on the way out he says to me, with an air of trusting confidence 'You'll be getting me some more of those Alex Rider picture books, won't you, Jane?'

'With a bit of luck,' I tell him.

Many thanks to Walker Books who provided a wonderful selection of much-enjoyed books for the Reading Club, and a set of Alex Rider graphic novels for Luke.

YOUR REGULARS

BLAME IT ON THE BOSSA NOVA

Ian McMillan

'm writing this in silence. Of course that's not true. Listen: my fingers tapping on the keyboard; the washing machine's minimalist music; Mr. Lowe next door's radio playing opera muffled by brick and wallpaper; a motorcycle zooming by on the main road; the dog barking up the street; an almost undetectable ice-cream van chiming far away; the clock; a toilet flushing; a blackbird's alarm call.

Somehow I block the noises out as I write. Of course that's not true: I sublimate the noises, mix them in to my thinking like you mix Carnation Milk into jelly. As I write they're there, somewhere, like aural fossils.

My first memories of writing as a child are of writing to sound; as I sat and filled exercise books with outlandish adventures on the planet Loki my mother would be listening to Radio 2 or later, Radio 4 and my dad would be singing songs like 'The Old Rugged Cross' and 'Donald Where's Yer Troosers' as he washed up noisily. And somehow, in ways that I couldn't define, the sound helped the writing. Somehow the rhythms of the singing and Andy Stewart's instinctive storytelling shaped the things I was scribbling; they didn't distract, they did the opposite of distract: they attracted. They attracted ideas to them which I rushed to get down on paper as they filtered through the music or the speech.

IAN McMILLAN

This carried on as I got older. When I wrote I liked a bit of noise; the radio, the television, the kids growing up and listening to and watching the things they loved. Poems were written to the sound of Pugwall and Johnny Briggs and Take That and Blur. When I talked to other writers I found that I was a little unusual; a lot of writers didn't like a soundtrack, they liked silence (or the version of the silence that I describe in the first paragraph) so they sat in a study or a room with a shut door and the 'silence' helped the words to come.

So I tried the silent approach; after all, I was a proper writer making a living from my pen so I had to make enough dosh to keep us all in Take That albums and vegetables. We had the loft converted into a room by chaps with tinny radios who whistled along to the tunes. When it was finished I ascended the ladder like a distorting mirror image of Neil Armstrong clambering down to the Moon. That's one small step for Ian, one giant leap for Ian's writing. I poked my head up into the loft and I breathed in the quiet. And the dust, which made me cough.

I sat in the loft. The aforementioned dust hung in the sunbeams as though it was a representation of all the poems and plays and film scripts I was going to write in that room. Downstairs I could just about hear the sounds of life: my girls had their mates around and they were laughing and singing. Overhead, a helicopter sliced the air. I coughed again. I got out my laptop. I stared at it like I was looking at it for the first time. I sipped my tea and was amazed at the sound my slurp made in the lit semi-silence of my writing chamber.

I lasted an hour. A long, dragging, empty hour during which I tickled the keyboard a couple of times and made a few primitive rune-like scratchings in my notebook.

And then I went downstairs and rejoined the human race and since then I've written downstairs, first at the table (clearing the stuff away when it was time for tea) then at a temporary white fold-up table that I stupidly left in the middle of the back room for about a year, making people walk round it, until I decided to fold it up every night, and now at a table in the corner of the room. Near the sounds. Near the life.

I don't listen to music any more as I write, though. I used

to: Radio 3 with its wonderful mission to inform, educate and entertain; jazzradio.com, particularly its Avant Garde channel; Accuradio's many jazz channels; podcasts and CDs. I found that, like my mother's radio and my dad's singing, they helped me to think, helped me to negotiate grammar and euphony and spot the false trails and cracked sounds in a narrative.

I'm 57. For the last few years, as my fifties took hold like a muffler tightening round my ageing neck, I've found that music can be that distraction it never was before, that it's no longer an attracting force. I end up listening to it which means I'm no longer listening to the music of my words. I tap my feet to a piano trio rather than trying to breathe lines into some kind of life, some authenticity beyond pop-up and temporary exhibition.

So now, reluctantly, it's just the non-silence of Mr Lowe's radio and the distant ice-cream van as I write. Which is good, because it leaves the avant-garde music and the Mixcloud sounds and the radio dramas and the stories to be listened to properly. A real experience rather than a soundtrack. Foreground not background. And sometimes, I reckon, my listening still informs my writing: a particular sentence can be traced back, forensically and archeologically, to a bossa nova tune I heard last Friday.

Blame it on the bossa nova? That's one small step.

YOUR REGULARS

DISTRACTION

Enid Stubin

he New Illness Etiquette' – you know from this? I may have been in line at a Duane Reade, New York's ubiquitous discount-drugstore chain, when the old illness etiquette was retired, but a spate of books has appeared about handling someone else's bad news with wisdom and grace. Will Schwalbe's *The End of Your Life Book Club* recalls his mother's struggle with pancreatic cancer and the reading that distracted and delighted them both. Letty Cottin Pogrebin's *How to Be a Friend to a Friend Who's Sick* mixes memoir and self-help, with an account of Pogrebin's own treatment for cancer and chapters titled 'Everything I Know I Learned in the Waiting Room'.

As someone who doesn't mind hospitals, I see the point of this emerging genre. To the larger population articulating profound horror at what goes on inside hospitals, a terror of the way they smell, I nod: that's just how I feel about hair salons. But in a hospital, people get better; really smart, if socially inept, doctors fix things, and nurses care for patients with compassion and skill. The rational side of me blossoms, and I figure the news is likely to be good. There's definitely a protocol, and I'm not bad at it.

Someone's having a 'procedure' and needs a note-taker or an 'escort' back home; a spouse or sister or parent faces hours in a waiting room and might like some company. We get the call and arrive on time, in the right hospital wing, having found the correct elevator bank. And we take along small bills and change for the vending machines, a notebook for doctors' and radiologists' names, and a book, perfect props. Research might also be welcome: asked about the cardiac surgeon, my own internist had weighed in. 'Not the best in the city. Not the best in the country. The best on the planet. And a nice guy.'

Armed with this information, I arrived at the Mount Sinai family waiting room, an upscale corporate lounge outfitted with computer carrels and a machine that dispensed half a dozen exotic blends of coffee and eight simpering herbal teas, all interchangeable. Claude had already been taken to the operating room, and Joanna was sitting in a chair and leafing through the *New York Times*. I'd brought my low-end cell phone and *Behind the Beautiful Forevers*, Katherine Boo's meditation on a Mumbai slum, but hesitated to open it. And why would I, when on the coffee table were multiple copies of *New Beauty*, a physician-endorsed magazine that saw no $200 face cream as too expensive and no surgical cosmetic procedure as *de trop*? Upholding this enlightened editorial stance, *New Beauty* presented page after glossy page of breakthrough treatments (the pearl facial, the diamond facial, the vampire facial), advertisements that dovetailed with the practices of the plastic surgeons who hawked the questionable products and services, and gorgeously inane features on luxe liposuction pilgrimages to Singapore. We had fun surveying the $800 moisturizers and cackling over the $1,000 serums, not quite sure what anything actually did but happy to lose ourselves in this wholehearted appreciation of the trivial. Much better to consider the advisability of blepharoplasty in conjunction with a well-timed face lift than imagine the graphic details of the aortic heart-valve replacement Joanna's husband was having at the moment.

Rich and strange as *New Beauty* proved, we did come to the end of the issue, and I picked up Joanna's discarded *Times*, shuffling to the New York pages I consider my personal gossip sheet. That morning provided a delicious tidbit: the president of the American Academy of Arts and Sciences, a 233-year-old outfit that elects to its august membership the movers and shakers of the English-speaking world, had been caught padding her résumé. Acquainted with the lady from graduate school, I yelped in delighted recognition and launched into a lively account of her relinquishment of literary study and subsequent ascent of the administrative ladder, at one point attaining the position of Vice President for Academic Affairs (you can't make this stuff up). Alas, despite her glittering trajectory, which included marriage to two dreary academics, she hadn't actually been granted the doctorate in literature listed on her CV – a problem. Joanna found the whole story rollicking or was good enough to pretend to enjoy my tales from the Downstairs Maid School of Literary History. At that point Claude had been in surgery for three hours, and amusement was my aim.

One can't always count on kismet, but that was a good day for academic scandal. Under the circumstances, important contemporary nonfiction wasn't really on; paper cups of French roast and high-level university tittle-tattle were. By the time Joanna heard her name called and was summoned to a phone call from the surgeon, we'd exhausted the reading material in the waiting room. The doctor's news was good and even better, and within a few hours she and her son Nick saw Claude in recovery. We went off to celebrate in high style at a diner where souvlaki hobnobbed with Sicilian specialties on a hefty Naugahyde menu. Inconsequentiality rather than serious reading had filled the scary hours.

One of my cultural heroes is Joseph Severn, the young painter who got talked into accompanying Keats to his 'posthumous life' in Italy. For a seminar in Romantic literature, I read each of three sizable biographies within a couple of weeks, and somehow I inevitably reached each writer's account of the shattering death in Rome at four a.m., when my father would be up and about, preparing his breakfast of instant coffee, toast, and farmer cheese. The sound of my snuffling cut into his early-morning solitude. What was I crying about? Keats's despair at what he recognized as the relentless progress of his disease; the poignancy of his efforts at cheerfulness; the agony brought forth by Severn's well-intentioned but clumsy ministrations – 'Don't breathe on me – it comes like ice'; and his compassion for the hapless nurse he would leave behind – 'I pity you poor Severn – what trouble and danger you have got into for me.' Severn might endure throughout literary history as a patsy, a lightweight, ambitious striver who got more than he'd bargained for, a slight sensibility entrusted with the care of a brilliant poet, but he was 'there', as the caregivers say, and because of him we have our dying Keats.

A good friend has gotten a rotten diagnosis, and while I'm genuinely hopeful about the outcome, what Dee could use from me are time and tact, including chatter about anything but biopsy, staging, insurance forms, scheduling, tests, and surgery. In an effort to divert, I acted out a scene for her. Asked by a cousin at a family dinner, 'What should I read next?' I suggested D. H. Lawrence's *Sons and Lovers*. 'Oh yeah? Why?' Warming to my task, I described Mrs. Morel's triumphant arrival home from marketing with the flowered dish she'd haggled for and the clump of muddy pansies ready for planting, the conspiratorial excitement kindled in her son Paul, the admixture of guilt and elation at having spent household money on inessentials. 'No, no, no!' my prospective reader wailed, clapping her hands over her ears and chanting to drown out my voice. 'I *hate* knowing the details of a book I haven't read yet'.

'Well,' Dee shrugged, philosophical, 'that's the difference between reading and loving books.' She paused, smiling. 'Cornflowers.'

'What?'

'The flowers on the dish she takes home. Cornflowers.'

It's just a word, I know. But it summoned a shared moment of recognition: a mother and son huddled over a shard of beauty in their hardscrabble life, a glimpse of loveliness alongside the thudding anxiety. Dee knows something about Lawrence's 'bright book of life,' the specificity that calls the natural world into focus for us. I thought of the phrase that ends 'Prayer' (I), George Herbert's sumptuous catalog of worldly preoccupation and spiritual insistence: 'Something understood'.

YOUR REGULARS

ASK THE READER

Brian Nellist

Q What does the term 'classic' mean as applied to English literature? Reviews of new novels and blurbs adorning their covers regularly use it, indeed so frequently that I'm amazed to be living through a 'classic' period. It doesn't feel like that.

A I recognise your slight irritation but anything that actually gets people reading books becomes I think admissible on the grounds of general utility. Dr Johnson uses the term not of a specific book but of writers to mean 'an author of the first rank' and for him what confers such status is not so much personal taste as time, the survival of value in a work through all the changes of circumstance, outlook and culture that historical change brings about. Just as for Darwin the decisive factor in the survival of species is environmental change so for this older cultural definition of a 'classic' it is time itself. C. S. Lewis reviewing his friend Tolkien's *The Hobbit* commented 'Predictions are dangerous: but *The Hobbit* may well prove a classic'. T. S. Eliot addressing the Virgil society in 1944 makes a cognate point but one which I find very heartening. It is the nature of such writing not to be dependent on the knowledge of scholars. Rather, anyone 'can try to offer, for the general use, the benefit of whatever wisdom Virgil may have helped them to acquire, in relation to their own experience of life'. Much contemporary fiction is written with such inventiveness, vitality of voice, range of insight that it deserves the praise it gets but whether it will be found to be 'classic' is an honour that no single critic can bestow but must be left to the stern censorship of time.

I say 'stern' because we must not endow time with any particular perception. Presumably the reason we have so many more plays by Euripides than Aeschylus is that one was more popular in late Antiquity than the other. Manuscripts are vulnerable. It's by accident that two of the greatest English medieval poems, *Sir Gawain and the Green Knight* and *Pearl*, survive in a single volume. If it were not for the activities of Heming and Condell most of Shakespeare's plays would not be known to us other than as passing references in documents of his day. The problem with print is that so much past writing occupies our bookshelves that the idea of a 'classic' becomes scarcely tenable without the aid of barbarian invasions that would force us to save the works we could not live without. Outside that comparatively small number of writers there is no canon in English. I have a one-volume *Corpus Poetarum Latinorum*; the idea of a comparable work for English poetry is an impossibility. The threat of the canon was an idea invented quite recently by groups who thought their special interests had been excluded from the prevailing discussion.

What interests me in the analogy with the ancient Classics is how exclusive our use of the term classic has become. You're right, we use the term for prose fiction. We don't read of the classic histories of Simon Schama or the classic philosophy of Thomas Nagel or the classic essays of Oliver Sacks, the equivalents of Herodotus or Aristotle or Plato. The old Everyman's library of Ernest Rhys was less exclusive and Penguin books have used the term inclusively for, well, say Sir Charles Lyell's *Principles of Geology*. He wrote better, more imaginatively than Darwin; come on, who could resist someone who called geology 'the autobiography of the earth'? So if now I'm on the subject of writers and books neglected because, though insightful, life-enhancing, written with vivacity, they don't belong to our dominant categories then the field is open and space will have to stop me. Why always do we get Newman's *Apologia* but never his mind-opening *Grammar of Assent* or his *University Sermons*, the greatest pulpit writing in two-hundred years? Thanks to Penguin for George MacDonald's *Fairy Tales* but Everyman used to issue *Phantastes* whereas you have to find *Lilith*, his greatest work, with difficulty. Even with novels every forty years or so publishers realise that George Gissing and Mark Rutherford (Hale White) have gone AWOL and what about *Peter Wilkins*, Robert Paltock's entrancing answer to *Robinson Crusoe* and *Gulliver's Travels*?

'Hold on', you'll say, 'we can all name books we think neglected and the list would be long.' I agree; I got waylaid by novels whereas to come back to the point of that extension of our exclusive categories by the model of antiquity I sometimes curse the scholarly industry which transforms great writing into highly expensive editions heavy with annotations of works that should otherwise increase the joy of nations. The letters of Cicero and Seneca are readily available to any reader of Latin but the personal writing of Pope, Johnson, Cowper, Keats, Byron sees the sun but rarely and, as I say, basically in volumes that frown at the unprofessional reader. We need more 'Classics', more books to surprise, stimulate, move us out of our immediate comfort zone. My dog goes around the house with a stuffed draught-excluder in his mouth because he's bored. Too much of our reading operates like that; let the draughts blow in.

YOUR RECOMMENDATIONS

FEATURING FIVE
NOVELLAS

Angela Macmillan

I am not sure I like the term novella as it seems to suggest light reading. The long list of famous novellas or short novels includes *Heart of Darkness, The Death of Ivan Ilych, Of Mice and Men, The Strange Case of Dr Jekyll and Mr Hyde, Ethan Frome* to name a few mighty books with nothing light about them. Over the next two issues I shall be recommending a variety of books all of which, though only one hundred or so pages, are examples of works that are neither over-extended short stories, nor poorly fleshed-out novels, but good books which have found their own perfectly balanced and economically concentrated form.

Willa Cather, *O Pioneers*
Dover Thrift ISBN-13: 978-0486277851

Against the historical background of the great American pioneers struggling to tame the new land, Willa Cather tells the story of Alexandra Bergson whose life on a Nebraskan farm is willingly dedicated to the harsh prairie and to preparing the way for future generations. She is a true heroine; an elemental figure, independent and resourceful, at one with land she lives in: 'With her free step, her upright head and calm shoulders, she looked as if she had walked straight out of the morning itself'. The frontier is not a place entirely governed by the strongest and fittest; Cather shows it to be a place where the finest human qualities rather than greatest physical strength make the difference.

J.L.Carr, *A Month in the Country*
Penguin Classics ISBN-13: 978-0141182308

In his dedication J.L.Carr quotes Dr Johnson, 'A novel: a small tale, generally of love'. In the hot summer of 1920, Tom Birkin, a shell-shocked survivor of The Great War, comes to an Oxfordshire village to uncover a medieval mural in the village church. As he painstakingly peels off the layers of centuries of paint and dirt so, slowly, he begins to heal and reconnect to life. The book has an elegiac feel, for even as Birkin uncovers the past so a way of life in a rural village is slipping away forever. Tender and profound, this bittersweet novel, generally of love, nevertheless acknowledges the frailty of happiness and the brevity of life.

Carson McCullers, *The Ballad of the Sad Café*
Penguin Classics   ISBN-13: 978-0141183695

A sad story which ends bleakly. So why read it? Because it is about love and the consequences of living without it. Miss Amelia, 'A dark, tall woman with bones and muscles like a man', slightly cross-eyed and reclusive falls deeply in love with Cousin Lymon, a malicious, swaggering hunchback who, in turn, becomes obsessed with 'bold and fearless and cruel' Marvin Macy, Miss Amelia's estranged husband. Amelia and Cousin Lymon open a café in her house which wonderfully brings to their remote little town a sense of community and pride. But just as it is born of love, so it is destroyed. A strange, beguiling prose ballad in which comedy and tragedy come disturbingly close.

Margaret Oliphant, *The Library Window: A Story of the Seen and the Unseen*
Kindle Edition

Here is such a haunting, baffling story of a girl increasingly seeing further and further into a possibly unreal window in the house opposite and then alarmingly losing the revelation. Mrs Oliphant is a great nineteenth-century realist writer but this tale, one of her last and written shortly after the death of her two remaining children, inhabits the very margins of life and death and is at once realist and visionary. It is haunted by images of reading and writing. The meaning is perhaps ungraspable though that is not as important as the attempt to do so.

Tobias Wolff, *The Barracks Thief* **from** *The Stories of Tobias Wolff*
Bloomsbury ISBN-13: 978-0747531531

Unusually for a short novel this superbly crafted story is told from multiple points of view but centres on a young man thoughtlessly joining the US Army and training for service in Vietnam. Occasionally crude and uncompromising, it is finally powerful in its persuasion toward a fuller understanding of motive rather than narrow-minded judgment. Tobias Wolff knows and shows how with time we might get over and through bad experience and how casually we rewrite our personal history.

A LITTLE *MORE* ALOUD

WILKIE COLLINS
ARMADALE

Selected by Angela Macmillan

Armadale *is a riveting mystery novel with a plot too complicated to summarise here. Suffice to say that the naïve Allan Armadale who has never known wealth before has inherited the considerable estate of Thorpe Ambrose in rather dubious circumstances. In this scene he walks in his garden for the first time and discovers the sixteen-year-old daughter of one of his tenants. If you read this hugely entertaining novel you will meet one of the darkest female characters in nineteenth century literature. Lydia Gwilt is a bigamist, a drug addict and a poisoner; a monster but a human being, always.*

Allan descended the terrace steps in front of the house, whistling cheerfully. He had met the serious responsibility of settling his domestic establishment to his own entire satisfaction. 'People talk of the difficulty of managing their servants,' thought Allan. 'What on earth do they mean? I don't see any difficulty at all.' He opened an ornamental gate leading out of the drive at the side of the house, and, following the footman's directions, entered the shrubbery that sheltered the Thorpe Ambrose gardens. 'Nice shady sort of place for a cigar,' said Allan, as he sauntered along with his hands in his pockets. 'I wish I could beat it into my head that it really belongs to *me*.'

The shrubbery opened on the broad expanse of a flower garden, flooded bright in its summer glory by the light of the morning sun.

On one side, an archway, broken through, a wall, led into the fruit garden. On the other, a terrace of turf led to ground on a lower level, laid out as an Italian garden. Wandering past the fountains and statues, Allan reached another shrubbery, winding its way apparently to some remote part of the grounds. Thus far, not a human creature had been visible or audible anywhere; but, as he approached the end of the second shrubbery, it struck him that he heard something on the other side of the foliage. He stopped and listened. There were two voices speaking distinctly – an old voice that sounded very obstinate, and a young voice that sounded very angry.

'It's no use, miss,' said the old voice. 'I mustn't allow it, and I won't allow it. What would Mr. Armadale say?'

'If Mr. Armadale is the gentleman I take him for, you old brute!' replied the young voice, 'he would say, "Come into my garden, Miss Milroy, as often as you like, and take as many nosegays as you please." ' Allan's bright blue eyes twinkled mischievously. Inspired by a sudden idea, he stole softly to the end of the shrubbery, darted round the corner of it, and, vaulting over a low ring fence, found himself in a trim little paddock, crossed by a gravel walk. At a short distance down the wall stood a young lady, with her back toward him, trying to force her way past an impenetrable old man, with a rake in his hand, who stood obstinately in front of her, shaking his head.

'Come into my garden, Miss Milroy, as often as you like, and take as many nosegays as you please,' cried Allan, remorselessly repeating her own words.

The young lady turned round, with a scream; her muslin dress, which she was holding up in front, dropped from her hand, and a prodigious lapful of flowers rolled out on the gravel walk.

Before another word could be said, the impenetrable old man stepped forward, with the utmost composure, and entered on the question of his own personal interests, as if nothing whatever had happened, and nobody was present but his new master and himself.

'I bid you humbly welcome to Thorpe Ambrose, sir,' said this ancient of the gardens. 'My name is Abraham Sage. I've been employed in the grounds for more than forty years; and I hope you'll be pleased to continue me in my place.'

So, with vision inexorably limited to the horizon of his own prospects, spoke the gardener, and spoke in vain. Allan was down on his knees on the gravel walk, collecting the fallen flowers, and forming his first impressions of Miss Milroy from the feet upward.

She was pretty; she was not pretty; she charmed, she disappointed, she charmed again. Tried by recognised line and rule, she was too short and too well developed for her age. And yet few men's eyes would have wished her figure other than it was. Her hands were so prettily plump and dimpled that it was hard to see how red they were with the blessed exuberance of youth and health. Her feet apologised gracefully for her old and ill fitting shoes; and her shoulders made ample amends for the misdemeanour in muslin which covered them in the shape of a dress. Her dark-gray eyes were lovely in their clear softness of colour, in their spirit, tenderness, and sweet good humour of expression; and her hair (where a shabby old garden hat allowed it to be seen) was of just that lighter shade of brown which gave value by contrast to the darker beauty of her eyes. But these attractions passed, the little attendant blemishes and imperfections of this self-contradictory girl began again. Her nose was too short, her mouth was too large, her face was too round and too rosy. The dreadful justice of photography would have had no mercy on her; and the sculptors of classical Greece would have bowed her regretfully out of their studios. Admitting all this, and more, the girdle round Miss Milroy's waist was the girdle of Venus nevertheless; and the passkey that opens the general heart was the key she carried, if ever a girl possessed it yet. Before Allan had picked up his second handful of flowers, Allan was in love with her.

THE READER CROSSWORD

Cassandra

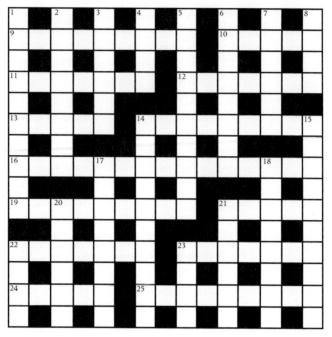

ACROSS

9. A step as an alternative for feet (9)
10. Synthetic fibre found in shorts or long trousers (5)
11. International organisation naïve and harmful to the environment (7)
12. Gave instructions as arranged (7)
***13 and 3 down.** They don't remember reordering lost tea rose (5, 6)
14. Ralph wandered off to dine and engage in flirtation (9)
***16.** Periods of bliss for Arthur? (6, 2, 3, 4)
19. Pike's chief in the vanguard (9)
21. Grave nuisance harbouring Barnaby's bird (5)
22. Toilets designed for ironical understatement (7)
23. Heavenly king creates prophet (7)
24. Expert fiend? (5)
***25.** See 22 down

DOWN

1. Hospital departments provide cursory links (10)
2. Mechanical devices are a product of German tragedy (8)
***3.** See 13 across
***4.** See 7 down
5. Linked to relative (10)
6. Audacious type! (8)
***7, 17 and 4 down.** Our poet circulated droll sonnets about Dean Fry (6, 4, 8)
***8.** Dine out with one of 7's ladies (4)
14. Declaration of vocation (10)
15. Create new life from a green tree (10)
***17.** See 7 down
18. He makes things, and sometimes makes them up (8)
20. Inter has Ben and Tom playing (6)
21. Identity manifest (6)
***22 and 25 across.** Her whole life is one of reflection (4, 2, 7)
23. Morse symbol of panache? (4)

*Clues with an asterisk have a common theme

BUCK'S QUIZ

THERE ARE FAIRIES AT THE BOTTOM

Angela Macmillan

1. In this novel, four children tell no one when their parents die.
2. Who sees 'Away behind the current row/Where no one else but cook may go,/Far in the plots, I see him dig,/Old and serious, brown and big.'?
3. In which book did the lover of H.G. Wells and cousin of Katherine Mansfield write about her life on her first husband's Pomeranian estate?
4. Who saw that, 'In the farthest corner of the garden was a tree quite covered with lovely white blossoms. Its branches were golden and silver fruit hung down from them, and underneath it stood the little boy he had loved'?
5. Who writes of this lush garden, 'Stumbling on melons, as I pass,/Ensnared with flowers, I fall on grass'?
6. Who finds a girl called Hatty in an unusual garden?
7. Where to find, 'Groves where rich trees wept odorous gums and balm,/Others whose fruit burnished with golden rind/Hung amiable'?
8. 'She is coming, my life, my fate;/The red rose cries, 'She is near, she is near.' Who is coming?
9. In which recent novel does a survivor of wartime Japanese atrocities turn to a former gardener to the Emperor of Japan to help her create a memorial garden to her sister?
10. 'A garden is a lovesome thing. God wot!' Yet who contends that God is not in it?
11. Who encounters deadly belladonna in the garden of Brandham Hall in 1900?
12. Which short story, first published in 1925 ends, 'and she went away, supposing him to be the gardener'?

PRIZES

The winner of the Crossword (plucked in time-honoured tradition from a hat) will receive a book prize courtesy of Vintage Classics, and the same to the winner of the fiendishly difficult Buck's Quiz.

There were no winners this time!

Please send your solutions (marked Cassandra Crossword or Buck's Quiz) to The Reader Organisation, The Friary Centre, Bute Street, Liverpool, L5 3LA. The deadline for answers is 11 October, 2013.

ANSWERS

CASSANDRA CROSSWORD NO. 42

Across

7. Faction **8.** Rostova **10.** Knight **11.** Exemplar **12.** Anna **13.** Leo Tolstoi **14.** War and Peace **19.** Caballeros **22.** Mark **23.** Karenina **24.** Errant **25.** Wheesht **26.** Remarks

Down

1. Dawning **2.** Stigmata **3.** Mortal **4.** Dovecote **5.** Stopes **6.** Aviator **9.** Second trial **15.** All right **16.** Cambrian **17.** Natasha **18.** Vronsky **20.** Aretes **21.** Scenes

BUCK'S QUIZ NO. 50

1. Joseph, *Wuthering Heights* **2.** Arthur Seaton, *Saturday Night and Sunday Morning* **3.** Mary and Martha in *The Secret Garden* **4.** Nicholas Nickleby **5.** Billy Liar **6.** Coal mining **7.** Margaret Hale, *North and South* **8.** 'Resolution and Independence' **9.** *Sons and Lovers* **10.** William Woodruff, *The Road to Nab End*

FICTION

URCHIN

Victoria Benn

The first thing he notices is the shape of the grey snaking branches above him as he looks through the triangular opening of the tent, against a sky of brightest blue. The second thing he notices is his mother, walking away from him, into the foaming sea.

The boy is sullen. Inclined to be. He has reason and his reasons concern the fact that he wants a world. A smooth round globe, blue as the oceans, that he can hold in his hand. What he doesn't want is the messiness of people walking away from him, things trailing off. He wants a world to hold, that is as perfect as one of his mother's pots. Yellowed, flecked with coruscations and oxidised pits, like the surface of the moon. Within his mother's pots, as with the moon, there exist microcosms. Self-contained worlds that are bound, and beautiful for that. This is what he most wants. Everyone needs a world. Don't they?

* * *

Tomi's mother is beautiful. Her hair flies up in thick black strands as she walks to the surf, wrapped in a sarong. This image, from several weeks ago now, is burned into Tomi's brain. He thinks back to the camping trip. Tomi would build a fire in the mornings and his mother would cook fish. Tall smooth buildings of flesh coming apart in neat sections. Boiled rice. The simplicity of these meals pleased them both. They talked a bit and laughed. His mother liked to explore the rocky outcrops below the headlands. Jumping from rock to rock, not wishing to stay still, she quickly outpaced him. Perhaps Tomi did not want to keep up, preferring to linger at the rockpools, thorny black urchins with dank purple aureoles retreating at the touch of his finger.

He cannot remember when he first noticed his mother's beauty. Now he is aware that it keeps them apart. Her smooth, laughing beauty, always augmented by fabrics and beads, it seems to Tomi, is what carries her away. Keeps her out late. Makes her distracted.

Now, he looks in the mirror and is repelled by what he sees. Japanese. Not enough that in Japan he might be considered beautiful. There, instead of looking Japanese, he is aware of his father's European features, reflected in his own face. Here, he just feels ugly. He is most grateful for his freckles; those biscuity flecks scattered over his nose and cheekbones. 'You could pass for Australian', his friend Paul once said. What else am I? He remembers thinking this. In Japan I'm a foreigner. Gaikoku-jin. But he didn't say this. You don't tell a sandy-haired surfer about being Australian. It would be different if Tomi went to a city school, where there are so many different faces, no-one looks the same. But not in this neck of the woods. Here, the blonde rule.

He has not seen Paul outside school for a while. Tomi is troubled by a mixture of feelings for his friend, best described as a sort of angry love. He has no idea how Paul feels, but once, he knows, they were close, spending all their time together, talking aimlessly, wrestling until they would collapse in a breathless heap.

It is late afternoon and these are the hours he finds hardest to fill. Later he will make himself something for dinner, unsure of when his mother will be home. Most afternoons she heads out to classes or openings, her red lipstick sometimes stuck with strands of hair as she opens the door into the wind. She often does not return until Tomi is in bed, asleep. He has recently started drawing. Intricate drawings, large in scale but finely detailed. He draws cities meticulously in graphite with occasional details in a rusty red ink wash. The cities are enormous with thousands of buildings of various sizes sandwiched together. Hints of people's lives are evident but few people are featured. Clothes lines are draped between high rise windows, their brittle black lines suggesting barbed wire. In a doorway a red splash draws the eye to a miniature figure, crumpled and perhaps bleeding. The cityscapes, for all their bleakness, are beautiful.

When he tires of drawing he decides to call Paul, ask him to come over. He knows he will say no. It has been almost a year since Paul has stayed here or since Tomi has been invited over. At school, Paul is friendly but distant. Makes excuses for why they can't catch up, sits with his other friends. Tomi has people to sit with but he somehow always finds his way to the art rooms where he finishes off his drawings. The worlds in these drawings are endless and labyrinthine and Tomi likes nothing more than to get lost in them, sometimes not noticing the bell that signals the end of lunch. Raku pots made by the other students line the walls, standing watch.

Paul's phone rings out so Tomi leaves the house to go walking. It is really this he most loves. Walking, slowly and without a reason, allows him to encounter the world in a way he seems to crave. He can make sense of the mass of lines and shapes he sees; hear the buzz of space around him. At the end of the road, the trees reach up to meet the power lines, which hum and crackle in conversation with the sky. Lines of perspective vanish into some meeting point obscured from vision. The light is falling now and down in the valley, Tomi sees the light in a kitchen window burning orange. The rectangle of light seems like a refuge from the vast, scattered air. He thinks with longing of Paul and his family in their sturdy white-walled home.

Paul's home is a pristine 1950's bungalow, which Tomi appreciates for its differences to his own 1970's timber and brick house. He used to like standing in his friend's meticulously maintained bathroom with its shining, square ceramic tiles in celadon green and rose pink. Quietly opening the mirrored cabinet with its green bevelled edges, looking inside. Just standing in this house that was not his, undisturbed. Paul's father had been a stentorian presence in the home. Tall, and watchful of the boys' every move, Paul himself was cautious around him but would also take opportunities to test his freedom where he could, smoking cigarettes out of the man's vision, or taking small amounts of money that wouldn't be missed.

Once, the boys had helped paint Paul's bedroom, using the smaller brushes to finish the cornices high up on the ceiling. Waiting till his father left the room, Paul gave Tomi a look to suggest some mischief was to follow. He took his brush and dipped it slowly in the glossy white paint. As his friend returned to his painting Tomi could see by his movements that he was working with precision, rather than with the broad, lazy brush-strokes they had been using. After some time his friend stood aside to reveal carefully painted obscenities in a neat but tiny script, the white paint bleeding into the undercoat as it dried. At school the next day Paul was quiet and as he took his seat delicately, Tomi knew he had been found out. It was strange that Tomi could no longer remember the words Paul had written, only his friend's ashen face as he sat in class.

Another time, the crime had been more grave. In Paul's room in the near dark, moonlight slanting on their faces, the boys grew brave. Tomi loved the way they could be so close, in a way not possible in daylight. Paul's warm breath, as he told some obscene joke, was sweet. Tomi could make out the outline of his friend's face, his squarish nose and sandy fringe softened in the moon's blue gleam. He asked what Tomi's name meant. He had, Tomi remembered, been the only friend who did not call him Tommy. Had taught others to say 'Toe-mee'.

'Shining sword', Tomi whispered into the dark, lying. He knew his name meant wealth, or plenty, but also that Paul would find this less interesting. The boys had both started to giggle, their bony frames shaking against each other. At night they explored each other's bodies, under the blankets, with a torch. Blunt fingers traced over ridges of ribs, their deep shadows as perfect as wind carved sand dunes. Further, their fingers testing the blue edges of places unseen. Later, they would lie with their awkward limbs entangled and it was in this way that Paul's father had found them, the bright electric light snapping on harshly, scattering shadows. The man's fury had been a slow burn and since that time Tomi has not returned to the house.

Tomi draws his eyes away from the window in the valley and begins to walk home. His mother's car is not in the drive when he returns and he wanders to the small workshop, set up in the breezeway, where she builds her pots. The space is still. He can feel the atoms shift and settle around him and for once he feels the need for noise, any noise that might disturb the useless vacuum of energy surrounding him.

He has the same feeling now that crept into the pit of his stomach one morning when he was dropped at school early – hours before he was supposed to be there. His mother had been in a hurry, had barely looked at him as she leant across to pull his door shut as he climbed out. It was dark and the boy stood still, watching the milky outlines of car lights on the distant highway, the shadowy shrubs alive around him. He was eight years old.

The feeling, or the memory, merges into another. Of Paul, last year, his arm raised lazily above his head, lying on the grass. The miraculous new growth of coarse, curling hair emerging in his armpit. Red, just pushing through the skin, and the faint but unmistakeable odour that the heat of the day brought forth. Tomi felt what he knew to be desire, mixed with a sadness he could not explain. The feeling had resurfaced when he had seen two older kids at school. It was a frosty morning and they sat close for warmth. Unaware they were watched, the boy had buried his nose in the girl's armpit, a gesture of intimacy that had alarmed and excited Tomi.

The memories dispel now as he walks towards the pots, picks up the largest and turns it in his hands. It is rough against his fingers and its colours are so subtle; a seamless shift from burnt gold to palest blue. It is almost perfectly spherical with a darker, uneven lip at the top. It looks somehow unfinished.

Tomi looks intently at the beautiful pot before he lets it smash to the ground with a satisfying crunch, its shape returning to its former sandy substance. He does not hesitate before smashing each and every pot he can find and when he has finished, the floor resembles a parched and blasted moonscape. He makes no sound but feels wet tear tracks on his cheeks, which he wipes away with shame.

The boy is in a deep sleep when he is woken by his mother in the night. His heart shifts him with force out of his dream, thudding heavily in his chest. His mother's face is not beautiful now, but looks every day of its age, grey and angry. Her voice is a strangled sound, thick with anger as she asks, again and again, 'What did you do?' Tomi tries to react but can only see his mother as a far off storm, a powerful force of electrical energy as remote and brilliant as the cascading solar flares of a distant sun. He observes her with wonder. She seems like a submerged sea creature behind the thick glass wall of an underwater observation tank. Slowly she is coming toward him and the sounds are starting to break through. His face is wet again but he seems to have no part in his tears. It is when his mother is beside him, crying and holding him, her breath warm in his ear, that he feels the sobs start to rise.

* * *

In the art rooms Tomi and Paul are working on their latest project, a series of Raku fired pots which have been decorated with the impressions of objects such as leaves and small seed pods. They are rough but Tomi finds pleasure in creating these objects, in arranging them along the shelving next to the other students' work. Paul has been friendlier these days but their old closeness is gone. Tomi sees now that Paul has simply been embarrassed by that earlier time in their lives and would rather forget it, but the sandy haired boy has sought Tomi's friendship and they are approaching something of their former ease together.

They walk home together, stopping to sit in the small park at the end of Paul's street. Dappled light from the trees falls on them as they talk aimlessly, telling some harsher joke that will mark them as emerging men. The tree against which Tomi leans is tall and the grey bark, its serrated edges thick like a scab, seems to harbour many secrets. He is left there for a moment alone as Paul waves him goodbye from the street above. There is a sense of calm now for Tomi, of time having passed, things having shifted. As he leaves he is struck by the colours of another tree, the bark of which has come away. The colours range from almost lime, fraying to soft russet rose, and in the shadows of dappled skin hides the flat blue of an unseen body part.

Tomi's mother has begun to spend more time at home but no, Tomi sees it is not going to be that kind of happy ending. He will need to grow up fast and move into the world, one day leaving her behind. Will he be watched, he wonders – as he has watched her walking into the foaming sea with her black hair flying up in ribbons – will he be watched? He remembers the fast train they once travelled on in Japan. He had been alarmed at the speed of the thing and could find no reference point on which his eye could rest, the country moving in a flash of greens and blues. Then he had looked up and seen the moon, pale as a shell and still, in the sky. He imagined the moon pulling the train along by force of its gravity, some invisible thread connecting them and keeping the train on its tracks. It was somehow calming, this silent disc in the sky that could watch over them, over it all. The train, the towns, the cities. The business of life and all its movement. It would be still and watch over them all. He would seek it out, wherever he went he would seek it out.

CONTRIBUTORS

Victoria Benn lives and teaches English in the Blue Mountains on the outskirts of Sydney. She writes when she can and has published both short fiction and theory in Australia. She has studied and taught sociology at Macquarie University.

Malcom Bennett keeps chickens and bees, and is frequently an embarrassment to his family. By way of a job, he studies zoonoses, the diseases that human animals get from non-human animals.

Josie Billington is Deputy Director of the Centre for Research into Reading, Information and Linguistic Systems (CRILS)

Martin Boston has been a long-time friend of *The Reader*. He was a much loved and respected teacher for many years. This issue is dedicated to his memory.

Charles Darby-Villis is RISE (Reading in Secure Environments) co-ordinator & Reader-in-Residence, HMP Low Newton, Durham.

Casi Dylan is Literary Learning Manager at The Reader Organisation, where she has worked since 2008. Born in Cwmystwyth, Ceredigion, she now lives in Glasgow although her work has taken her all over the UK as well as Denmark and Australia.

Barney Eden is a great fan of TRO and a very part-time writer, songwriter, and even it seems poet. In his other life he's an academic based in London.

Jonathan Edwards' first collection of poems will appear from Seren in 2014. In 2012, he won second place in the Cardiff International Poetry Competition and was commended in the Basil Bunting Award.

Stuart Evers' first fiction collection, *Ten Stories about Smoking*, won the London Book Award 2011 and his debut novel, *If This is Home*, was published by Picador to considerable acclaim in 2012. A graduate of the University of Liverpool, he now lives in London.

Seán Haldane is, by ancestry, something of a human compass: a quarter each English, German, Scottish and Irish. His poems are simply English. He has worked as a lecturer, part time farmer, small press publisher, psychotherapist, and consultant clinical neuropsychologist. He lives in London.

Mark Irwin was formerly Professor of English at the University of Kent and Chairman of the Thomas Hardy Society. His work on Hardy includes a full-length study: *Reading Hardy's Landscapes*. His third novel, *The Skull and the Nightingale*, appeared this summer.

Hannah Lowe is a poet and prose writer. Her first full collection *Chick* (Bloodaxe, 2013) is currently shortlisted for the Forward Best First Collection Prize. *Rx*, a chapbook of love poems is published later this year by sine wave peak.

Frances Macmillan is Senior Editor at Vintage, responsible for the Vintage Classics list. She began her career as an intern at The Reader Organisation.

Ian McMillan was born in 1956 and has been a freelance writer/performer /broadcaster since 1981. He presents *The Verb* on BBC Radio 3 every Friday night.

Alexis McNay is a Project Worker for Get Into Reading and a part of the TRO National Criminal Justice Team, reading regularly at HMP Kennet.

Bernard O' Donoghue is a Fellow of Wadham College, Oxford, where he teaches Medieval English. His most recent collection is *Farmer's Cross*, Faber and Faber 2011.

Jean Sprackland's fourth collection, *Sleeping Keys*, is published by Cape this autumn. *Tilt* was the winner of the Costa Award 2008. *Strands: A Year of Discoveries on the Beach* won last year's Portico Prize for Non Fiction. She is Reader in Poetry at Manchester Metropolitan University.

Enid Stubin is Assistant Professor of English at Kingsborough Community College of the City University of New York and Adjunct Professor of Humanities at NY University's School of Continuing and Professional Studies.

Dr Jane Thomas is Senior Lecturer in English at the University of Hull specialising in the work of Thomas Hardy and late Victorian literature and art. She is the Academic Director of the Biennial International Thomas Hardy Conference and Festival.

John Wedgwood Clarke is Leverhulme poet in residence at the marine biology department of the University of Hull. His first collection, *Ghost Pot*, will be published in October by Valley Press. He is also UK and Ireland poetry editor for Arc Publications.

Distribution Information

Trade orders Contact Mark Chilver, Magazine Department, Central Books

email: mark@centralbooks.com
web: www.centralbooks.com
tel: 0845 458 9925   fax: 0845 458 9912
Central Books, 99 Wallis Road, London, E9 5LN

All other queries regarding trade orders or institutional subscriptions
Contact The Reader Office

email: magazine@thereader.org.uk
tel: 0151 207 7207

SUBSCRIBE

Just £18 per year with Direct Debit

Either print off an order form from our website (www. thereader.org.uk), call us on 0151 207 7207 or email (magazine@thereader.org.uk) and we will send you a form in the post.

Cost by Cheque or PayPal:

UK   4 issues   £24.00   (including p&p)
Abroad   4 issues   £36.00   (including p&p)

Please make cheques payable to The Reader Organisation and post to: The Reader Organisation, FREEPOST RSSL-UHCB-EKKE, The Friary Centre, Bute Street, Liverpool, L5 3LA.

Don't forget to include your name and address, and the issue number with which you would like your subscription to begin.

Overseas readers: your cheapest method is by PayPal via our website: www.thereader.org.uk.

Please direct email enquiries to:
subscriptions@thereader.org.uk

the reader